The Librarian's Guide to

Book Programs
AND AUTHOR EVENTS

ALA Editions purchases fund advocacy, awareness, and accreditation programs for library professionals worldwide.

The Librarian's Guide to

Book Programs
AND AUTHOR EVENTS

BRAD HOOPER

An imprint of the American Library Association
Chicago | 2016

Brad Hooper is the former Adult Books Editor at *Booklist*. He is the author of two previous ALA Editions books, *The Short Story Readers' Advisory* (2000) and *Writing Reviews for Readers' Advisory* (2010). He was the 2015 recipient of the Louis Shores Award for outstanding reviewing. He served as Chair of the selection committee of the Carnegie Medals.

© 2016 by the American Library Association

Extensive effort has gone into ensuring the reliability of the information in this book; however, the publisher makes no warranty, express or implied, with respect to the material contained herein.

ISBNs
978-0-8389-1384-0 (paper)
978-0-8389-1398-7 (PDF)
978-0-8389-1399-4 (ePub)
978-0-8389-1449-6 (Kindle)

Library of Congress Cataloging-in-Publication Data

Names: Hooper, Brad, author.
Title: The librarian's guide to book programs and author events / Brad Hooper.
Description: Chicago : ALA Editions, an imprint of the American Library Association, 2016. | Includes bibliographical references and index.
Identifiers: LCCN 2016000487| ISBN 9780838913840 (print : alk. paper) | ISBN 9780838913987 (pdf) | ISBN 9780838913994 (epub) | ISBN 9780838914496 (kindle)
Subjects: LCSH: Libraries–Cultural programs–Handbooks, manuals, etc. | Reading promotion–Handbooks, manuals, etc. | Libraries and community–Handbooks, manuals, etc. | Libraries–Public relations–Handbooks, manuals, etc. | Book clubs (Discussion groups)–Handbooks, manuals, etc. | Public speaking. | Authors–Interviews. | Literary prizes.
Classification: LCC Z716.4 .H66 2016 | DDC 021.2–dc23 LC record available at https://lccn .loc.gov/2016000487

Book design by Kimberly Thornton in the More Pro and Proxima Nova typefaces.
Cover illustration © Rooster Stock/Shutterstock, Inc.

♾ This paper meets the requirements of ANSI/NISO Z39.48–1992 (Permanence of Paper).

Printed in the United States of America

20 19 18 17 16   5 4 3 2 1

CONTENTS

INTRODUCTION

Behind the curtain, I await the launch of the author program. I am within a couple minutes of being announced as the program moderator by the evening's master of ceremonies. There are five of us— four authors and I—standing in a line, in the order by which we will be announced and brought out onto the stage. We wait in silence as we hear the master of ceremonies extend his welcome to the audience and express his appreciation for their attending this event, and he promises it will be an educational, even exciting, hour and a half of listening to four noted authors discussing their writing lives.

All the authors are recognizably pros at this; I notice that not one is showing signs of nervousness. These four authors, their handlers, and ALA conference officials, along with me, had assembled in the "greenroom" only a half hour before, but that proved sufficient time for enough acquaintance to be established among us to achieve a degree of comfort for all of us; in other words, we were already a team. I had indicated to the ALA conference officials the order in which I would like the authors to speak, and that, of course, indicated the order in which we now stood backstage. The order of speaking determined the seating arrangement on stage, and that of course was important for allowing the sound technicians to follow the plan from backstage: meaning, they knew when to turn on and turn off mikes for each of the speakers.

Author number one is introduced, who then, as rehearsed, slips out from the curtains that are held apart by a stagehand at the back of the stage, and amid applause she takes her seat. Five big comfortable chairs have been arranged in a shallow U-shaped formation on the stage. Author number two, number three, and number four. And then I hear myself introduced.

I step out onto the stage and blink in the bright lights; it's like a TV studio. My sight quickly recovers and I find my chair, in the center of the "U," and sit down. I look out over an audience of 700 people. I momentarily freeze. "My goodness," I say to myself, "what have I agreed to do?" My well-rehearsed script, my knowledgeable preparation, abandons me for a second or two. High anxiety! Wouldn't I prefer doing anything else but this? Didn't the old adage that most people would choose a root canal over public speaking apply to me at this point?

There are few moments of dead reckoning as those you experience when walking onto a stage to come face-to-face with rows and rows of people staring intently at you, anticipating *your* performance. Public speaking, singing, acting, playing a musical instrument: all the same when it comes to the instant assault on your nerves from having to begin *your* performance immediately, because the launch of the program depends entirely on you, and is completely in your hands; nothing else can begin until you do. There can be no hiding now, no stepping back and letting events begin on their own. You tell yourself that most people in the audience are on your side, expecting your program to be wonderful, but then there is always that little voice in your head, telling you that there are always holdouts in an audience, and they don't expect much from you.

Once I've opened my lips and the few dry words that have gathered there are expelled from my desiccated mouth, I find that the next words emerge smoothly flowing, indicating to the audience that those few initial dry words have been "spit out" and now will be followed by smoothly gliding, safe and secure words that indicate I am in control of the program.

At this point, I am on my way to successfully maintaining the audience's attention for the next hour and a half. My comfort voice, which resides in the back of my mind, congratulates me on a successful lift-off, and being perpetually in my corner, it reminds me that I am aiming my program at various levels of interest in the audience, some eager and highly expectant of great results as well as those who will remain skeptical until nearly the end. My comfort voice says, "You'll want to score a direct hit at those skeptics, who assume they have nothing to learn here today." I am determined to prove those people wrong.

The above scenario is a typical situation faced by every public speaker, faced by every librarian who speaks before an audience, whether it is an audience of six individuals or six hundred individuals. This is particularly the situation of the typical librarian who finds herself, in the course of her readers' advisory and collection development duties, placed into a public speaking situation; being typical, the librarian often approaches such a situation armed with little experience in speaking before a group, large or small. Generally, librarians are untrained in public speaking because it is not part of the typical library science or information science curriculum. Nor is public speaking a particularly essential quality in a practicing librarian. The one-on-one connection with a library patron—the classic "reference interview"—does not count here. Comfort in that situation does not necessarily translate to an "at-ease" attitude when speaking publically.

The public speaking scenario I've just described to you was real. It actually took place, and new versions of that same basic program—with different authors, of course—have continued to take place at every Midwinter Meeting of the American Library Association. It is called the "Author Forum" and it occurs late Friday afternoon during Midwinter, just before the opening of exhibit hall, where it seems the entire publishing world is presenting their new wares in booths both large and small for the benefit of librarians attending the conference. The Author Forum program is more or less the official opening of the conference itself.

When I, as Adult Books Editor at *Booklist* magazine, found myself first invited to participate in an Author Forum almost twenty years ago, it represented what I had come to perceive, based on my experiences in various capacities of involvement in author programs, a low-level involvement. The folks at ALA's Conference Services invited publishers to submit names of relevant authors from their publishing pools that they would volunteer to send to the conference city. These author forum programs were of great repute and attracted huge audiences; consequently, publishers were glad to fund a trip to whatever city was the conference's location, usually as a promotional gesture for a new book that both author and publisher were eager to promote.

The Conference Services staff would then fall into step by looking over (again) the complete list of available authors, tracking a possible thematic connection between a small group of authors, and almost by magic pulling together a panel of, say mystery writers, or writers who had a book of theirs made into a movie, or a box-of-chocolates assortment of writers of genre fiction—from science fiction to thrillers to women's fiction to romance fiction. The Conference Services staff would perform all the behind-the-scenes work in honing the four individuals into a cohesive panel, and I will break the whole thing down for you in a later chapter. Part of this behind-the-scenes work, of course, is to inform the panel participants of the time limits on their personal contributions, suggest to them any special topics they should discuss, and, importantly, lay out the format of the panel for them. They would be called alphabetically to the rostrum by the moderator to present their "speech."

This is where I came in. My job as moderator was simple: introduce each panelist when their turn to speak came, and at the end of the whole program ask the audience for questions. My entire script, from general opening remarks to specific introductions for the individual authors, was written for me by the Conference Services staff. And more, it was printed out in large letters for easy reading, and I did not see the script—did not *need* to see the script—until I showed up in the greenroom forty-five minutes before the event and met the authors. I then read through the script during a five-minute quiet time in the corner of the room, and then—*voilà!*—I was ready to hit the stage.

In subsequent years, the event's format and presentation was changed. It got more complicated, yes, but that was all part of the improved quality. And my role as moderator certainly morphed into something more. A heavier burden was placed on my shoulders. And I loved it.

And what was the new format exactly? First, the seating arrangement on stage was altered. It now served to suggest—encourage—a conversation among the panelists as opposed to simply provide them with a place to park themselves before speaking. Seating, now, was in big, deep, luxurious chairs, like those you would want to curl up in to read. The arrangement of these chairs was still a shallow "U," with the moderator's chair the keystone in the arch. The set—the big, dynamically designed backdrop, in other words—went well beyond the stark nothingness that had back-dropped the speakers in former years.

The set now evoked a television studio set up for a talk show, with all the guests and the host to be on stage simultaneously. There was the kind of nuanced lighting like you'd find in a TV studio, muted here and spotlighted there to keep the eyes of the audience busy. And seating for the studio audience increased to accommodate 700 people. Word had gotten out that this Author Forum was becoming bigger and bigger business, with major-level writers on board, and a convention-wide consciousness had recently arisen and spread that said attendance at this event was the most special way for members to kick off the ALA Midwinter experience.

In the previous years of the Author Forum, there was a "greenroom" situated off to the side of the stage. But the greenroom was simply a smaller ballroom next to the much bigger ballroom in which the program itself was to be held. In the greenroom, the Conference Services people provided cold drinks, cookies, and fresh fruit. It was there I would meet the panelists, most of whom I'd not met before, and there too where I would be handed the script already composed for me. A cursory run-through on my own was sufficient.

Then the panelists and I unceremoniously marched to the next room, which was set up like an auditorium, and we made our way to the dais and took our assigned seats.

At the appointed time to begin, I arose, stepped over to the podium, greeted the audience in brief terms, and we were off and running. Once the last panelist had finished speaking, I bid my adieus to the panelists and went off to take care of my other Midwinter activities. "Glad I could help" pretty much summarized my attitude toward the program that had just taken place, my sense of accomplishment being at about the same level as the effort I had exerted. Not a great deal, in other words.

In the new "era" that now came upon us, which began in the mid-2000s, the greenroom was located in an actual room, which certainly went a long way to establishing the feel of a genuine greenroom—like one you undoubtedly would find in any TV studio. This room sat behind the stage, which meant one had to step around lots of technical equipment to get there. You noticed the quiet conditions immediately upon entering the room. Soundproofed? Seemed like it. In this "new era" greenroom, not only did I meet the panelists and their "handlers" but the panelists and I were also "miked"—meaning, to our lapels were affixed lavaliere microphones. That represented another big difference between the old and new era formats, and one that gave me a greater role in the program, and consequently drew out my sense of purpose and pleasure more intimately to its success or failure. Further, I now decided the order in which the panelists should speak, and the sound technicians went along with me; after all, the Conference Services staff designated me the "captain" of this enterprise and the tech crew were always looking to me for direction.

But the differences between the "old" and "new" eras of the Author Forum had only begun to surface. The conference staff's suggestion had been that the program should be a conversation among me and the panelists, hence the new seating arrangement onstage: comfy chairs for the panel and me. I supported this new arrangement wholeheartedly. I thought that the idea of all of us—panelists, me—sitting in large chairs in a semicircle was a stroke of genius. The Conference Services staff was shaking the Author Forum up and making it less formal.

A second aspect of the revised program, which was of course designed to make the Author Forum a less rigid production, came in the form of much greater moderator participation in how the program developed before the audience. "Developed" is the key word here. Every Author Forum since the inception of the "new" era version has become a distinctly unique and individual beast. No longer did the panelists arise one by one and walk to the podium to deliver a ten-to-fifteen-minute piece that hopefully had relevance to the program's intended theme.

I would now start with a panelist whom I already decided would be a good opener based on my familiarity with that person's published work. I conduct a ten-to-fifteen-minute interview; my questions need at least a two-or-three sentence response, but hopefully more. I hope the author lets my questions serve as a spark to ignite deeper memories and ideas and opinions that take the author into an interior place and allow him or her to bring out ideas and opinions and autobiographical details that do more than simply scratch the surface.

The program proceeds in that fashion. The second author easily follows the first, and then the third, fourth, and fifth. An important point to stress here is that I as moderator have to be quick on my feet, paying close attention to what the author is saying, which means not looking over my notes so closely as to call attention to the fact that I am looking things over. After all, by arranging the authors in the particular order you decided, you, as moderator, intended that your interviews would build upon one another, and that theme would emerge in the process and build a fine edifice. Now, what I'm going to suggest requires moderator dexterity: you as moderator must generate panelist-to-panelist conversation. The best way to encourage this is to actually ask the panelists for it. By the time you are interviewing your second author, you can, based on your close—naturally, right?—attention to the points made by the first author, compare what the second author is saying to the views of the previous author. With no trepidation, ask for a dialogue on the points of agreement and disagreement.

Now, I don't believe in raucous debate on any occasion, not even among family members around the Thanksgiving dinner table. And by *raucous* I mean voices getting elevated beyond a normal conversational level. Book-and-author programs are not *The McLaughlin Group* after all, with panelists taking on each other in mini-combat and slinging near insults far and wide. Remember that heated exchanges in front of people tend to embarrass onlookers. Not a good picture.

This cross-exchange among panelists undoubtedly will prompt one or more of them to add additional relevant information and can pose an intriguing question to the other panelists. As moderator, you cannot *force* an exchange; you never want to put a panelist on the spot by asking, for example, if he or she disagrees with something another panelist has said. Let me stress, dialogue between panelists should be genial and helpful to the purpose of the panel's theme and should contribute to a sense of team effort, not create a competition among the panelists and thus a division between them.

Need I say that politics has no place in the panel discussion? This is not a soapbox on which to stand to air blue state vs. red state matters, unless, of course, the authors are political writers and this is a politically themed panel. If this be the case, the moderator will understand that a more difficult task may lie before him: keeping the presentation and discussion from descending into argument. To help avoid that from happening, remind your panelists several times beforehand that they are "performing" today as *writers* about politics and should stay focused on the book(s) they wrote; and that this author forum is not an opportunity to broadcast one's views per se but is a place to discuss how the book they've written does that for them.

If conversation between two or more panelists does not take hold, it's not the moderator's fault. As I've said, a forced pitting of one panelist against another panelist will stand out as such and thus compromises the effectiveness—the appeal—of the program itself. You never want to appear as if you are starting a dog fight. But if conversation between or among the panelists—polite, sane conversation, that is—*does* take hold, the moderator's work is not over. The conversation must not only stay on topic, it also must stay within the time limit. Authors, especially when talking about themselves—their favorite topic—have a tendency to wander, to digress, to bring up from their only-too-easily-tapped-into remembrance far too many details for a four-author panel to handle. And discussing time restrictions brings up an age-old dilemma for a moderator: how to politely, without giving offense, let speakers know when they have gone over their allotted time and need to bring their contribution to a rather quick halt. There are good ways to do that, and we'll save the discussion about that issue for a later chapter.

So, basically what I'm saying is that creating and nurturing conversation among your panelists is like growing something in the garden: you want it to take root and thrive and make a very evocative covering of walks and open spaces but not grow so out of control that it's covering windows and climbing trees. But I can almost guarantee that whatever conversation springs up will soon die down on its own volition, and usually because the panelists never forget that the program you are presenting has had a rather strict format and is not a free-for-all. Like well-behaved children, they will draw themselves back into composure and, quietly, look again to you as the leader. Time to spark conversation again.

But remember, it takes just one such conversational flowering to create a good impression in your audience; one of their takeaways from the program will be the idea that there was an element of spontaneity in the proceedings. Too many such flowerings and the last speaker won't have time to give his or her full presentation and the audience will leave with the impression of bad planning.

Now, what exactly you as moderator should be asking your panelists, and whether to ask each one the same series of questions, will be addressed in a later chapter specifically addressing the topic of interviewing.

So, back to the program. You as moderator have completed your discussion with the final panelist. All conversation among the panelists has drawn to a close. You should have built into your time planning and management a ten-to-fifteen-minute question and answer session. The ALA Conference Services staff always accommodated that last but not least feature of the program by stationing two standing microphones out in the audience, for audience members to approach and pose a question to the panelist of their choice. The Q and A session is important for two reasons:

First, audience participation always leaves a good taste in the mouths of those who attend your program. It removes, to a degree, the barrier between audience and panelist; and that generates a "we're all just folks here" in the minds of the audience. It helps level the playing field. And the authors should be grateful they've been allowed to be there in front of the audience even more; people are more inclined to want to read the book of an author who, despite a glorious reputation, is "just like you and me."

Secondly, a Q and A session is beneficial to the moderator as a time to decompress, to sit back and let others more or less take the wheel. It's during the Q and

A session that you the moderator can bask in the glow of the great program you have wrought.

But the moderator is not quite finished. You must always thank the panelists by name for their participation and thank the audience for its attendance and participation.

There is nothing left to do now than to stand and acknowledge the applause and, in a single file, leave the stage for the greenroom, where everyone gets de-miked and congratulates one another on a very successful presentation.

May I name drop? Permit me to impart some of the celebrated authors I have "moderated" in the Author Forum and explain why I enjoyed them as panelists.

Susan Vreeland is an accomplished historical novelist who uses her love and knowledge of art history as the vehicle by which she explores the past in her fiction; in other words, her forte is the resurrection and reconstruction and imaginative "filling in" of major artists' lives and the significant works they were responsible for. Her most famous novel is *Girl in Hyacinth Blue* (1999), which offers as its compelling premise the successful ownership over the centuries of a Vermeer painting. In person, as a panelist on a book program, she presents herself as an elegant lady, seemingly shy at first but obviously, through her self-assured answers to questions about herself and her work, she is a person who possesses great sensitivity and is extremely articulate.

Remember the cycle of works, collectively titled *Tales of the City* by Armistead Maupin, which were made into a television series that became as much a cult favorite as the books upon which they were based? The novels—and then the TV series, too, of course—were set in San Francisco in the 1970s and 1980s and revolved around the friends and neighbors of one Anna Madrigal, a transgender back before transgenders were readily talked about—either in fiction or in public discourses. Maupin graced one of the Author Forum programs, and his anecdotes about his journalistic past—recalling how his editor at the newspaper where he'd worked would throw up his hands over Maupin always writing about things gay with "Gay, toujours, gay?"—and the making of the iconic TV series—remembering the loveliness and perfect casting of Olympia Dukakis as the key character Anna Madrigal— were priceless. And his enormity of spirit: at show's end, back in the greenroom his whispering to me, "It was *you* who led this program to its successful heights."

Ruth Ozeki is the author of high-end literary fiction, and in the wake of the big splash made by her beguiling novel *A Tale for the Time Being* (2013), she appeared on my Author Forum panel. Ruth has, of course, a website, and in my preparation of questions for her, I visited her website, and to my great pleasure I discovered a paean she'd written about librarians. So, my first statement to her, as we sat down on stage to begin the program, was that I'd found her "I love librarians" piece on her website. "So, Ruth," I encouraged her—admonished her—"tell our audience how much you care for them." She spoke eloquently about how important libraries and librarians have been to her. What an effective way to immediately win over an audience from the word go!

An engaging movie stemmed from Julie Powell's 2005 cooking memoir, *Julie and Julia*, the movie version carrying the same title. The book and subsequently the movie presented a very catchy premise. Powell felt bored and purposeless at her temp job in Manhattan, and to inject some meaning and interest in her life, she hit on a great—and time-consuming—idea, which was to cook all 524 recipes in Julia Child's classic *Mastering the Art of French Cooking*, all in one calendar year! Lots of people knew about her undertaking, because she kept a blog diary—one of the first instances of blogging. So, you do the math. Five hundred twenty-four recipes in Child's book, divided by 365 days in a year. Obviously, some days required handling more than one recipe; and the one technique of Child's that Powell dreaded and kept putting off was boning a chicken, which she ultimately did accomplish. As a participant on an Author Forum, she spoke about her Julia Child years but also about seeing her book turned into a movie, herself played by the delightful Amy Adams. From her remarks we learned that once movie rights have been sold, often—more often than not? More like usually?—the author is "relieved" of the book, as if having given it up for adoption, and the movie people turn it into the "person" they want it to be. But I did not gather from her comments that she felt any bitterness about the issue. Nor apparently toward the greatly negative press being garnered by her new book that had just been published, called *Cleaving*, about her adventures in learning the butcher's trade!

Mountain country, specifically the Two Medicines country, which, like Yoknapatawpha County in Faulkner's fiction in previous decades, serves as the customary fictional stomping grounds for the late novelist Ivan Doig, whose charm brought great buoyance to an Author's Forum a couple of years ago when he appeared on the panel to discuss what was then his most recent novel, *The Bartender's Tale* (2012), a historical novel about a bartender whose 12-year-old son came of age in his Daddy's saloon. The book is endearing in its warmth and humanity, admirable in its literary soundness. I'd not met Doig before we met in the greenroom, and he looked like he just might turn out to be intimidating. Nothing of the sort. Bearded, he looked professional, but at the same time like he might be a safari guide. As a panelist, he was a delight, giving answers to my questions readily and thoughtfully. In fact, he got so engaged in his presentation, he said at one point that his back would feel better if he perched on the arm of his big, cozy chair with his feet on the seat. No one, as far as I could tell, batted an eye. We were as engaged in his presentation as he was.

Praise be to the panelist who is polite, amusing, considerate of time (and what to do when they are *not* conscious of time we'll discuss in a later chapter), able to keep the comments on point, and able also to not be "hoggish" about audience attention. "Don't showboat" should be the mantra of every good book-program panelist.

As you have seen, the opening up of the panelists to expose personal anecdotes and somewhat private attitudes had been on the easy side. By all means, they are not all like that, and one in particular stays in my mind. I shall not name him, but let's call him Mr. Yes-and-No, because basically one-word answers were all I could elicit from him. But to the important subject of coaxing out from the reluctant answerer I will turn at a later chapter.

Remember, I am simply, in this introduction of my book, introducing you, the reader, with what I plan to share with you as all the pages, to the very last one, of this book are turned.

Essentially, what I will cover—what you will gain not only from my words but also from the first-hand experiences that stand behind the words—are many and widespread procedures and practices involved in producing or sponsoring programs and events by public, school, and special librarians that have the purpose of bringing together libraries, authors, and books for a meaningful encounter.

Chapter 1 will present my "feelings" about public speaking. Understand, the feelings will not be negative, for I thrill over public speaking. I will disabuse you of some of the hoary old maxims that are trumpeted to help you relax before a crowd; I will be honest about how much one's personality plays into success as a public speaker.

Chapter 2, my first stop in viewing the librarian in the capacity of organizer, facilitator, and participant in various types of book-and-author programs, starts off relatively simple. I discuss the librarian in a limited capacity: providing space for a local book club meeting. The event could be onetime only or regularly scheduled (as in monthly, in most instances). For these book clubs, the librarian would basically be only supplying a roof over the club's collective head. But we'll also talk about, within that context, the potential great public relations initiative that even such a bare-bones librarian participation can garner for your library.

The next step in our climb up the ladder of increasing librarian participation in a book and author program will be to place the librarian into a more direct host position for a book club. This would be a book club that the librarian organizes himself or herself: gathering interested book lovers in the community (and not necessarily limited to library patrons) into a regularly scheduled book club (meeting, of course, in the organizing librarian's library), or if participation interest is high, into two clubs meeting at different times (even discussing different books) so the group won't be so large as to inhibit spontaneous conversation. Yes, this situation is counterintuitive, because you might think that the larger the group, the more anonymous a participant might feel and thus not be shy about joining into the conversation. The opposite actually is true: the more people in a group, the more participants will experience performance anxiety, and the smaller the group the more relaxed and less conscious of "everyone staring at me" they will be. And, consequently, they will feel freer to add their comments and opinions about the book to the group conversation.

Whether the more-than-one grouping is fluid—meaning, people can attend this group or that group without being required to remain at all times in the Tuesday night group and not slide into the Thursday group—is up to the librarian-organizer. We'll discuss the pros and cons of such fluidity when the time comes—that is, when we reach the chapter covering this topic. And the librarian has another path open to them: serving as conversation leader himself or herself or having the group(s) elect their own. Again, there are pros and cons of each situation to be looked at later. If guest speakers are the way the book group wants to go, as an authority on the book at hand to either serve as conversation leader or as a "consultant" sitting in to add comments here and there and serve as a resource for any questions the members may have, if that's the way the club is constituted, then the librarian may help the group locate and invite the authorities, or at least aid someone in the club in their efforts to do so.

Chapter 3 will include guidelines for selecting books that would make successfully involving book-group discussions. Types will be discussed and specific titles suggested.

Upward we go on the ladder of drawing on the time and knowledge of the librarian in offering to the community a series of engaging book and author programs. Thus, in chapter 4, we arrive at a perennially popular form of such a program, one that the library can benefit from: the widespread demise of bookstores, which used to play host to these programs. I'm speaking of author readings, which I cover in chapter 4. Promotion is key here, of course, and places into which to reach to gain publicity for your program will be on our conversational plate. Book signings are always a pleasant conclusion to an author reading, and how to connect with the author's publicity handlers or a local bookstore—if there is one!—to get copies for the audience to purchase and the author to autograph will top off this chapter.

Now, in chapter 5, we move even higher in the level of library participation in books and author programming, to that which may test a librarian's moxie in public performance and will call on skills the librarian may feel are beyond his or her talents—but I will certainly disabuse the reader of such self-limiting sentiments. This category of program is centered on interviewing. Interviewing authors, that is, and the "bigger" the author the better. A local relatively unknown writer has its attraction, but people may not want to come out to hear a relative unknown be asked questions about his life and writing. On the other hand, authors whose books are always reviewed in the major review media, and authors that made the talk shows as part of their book tour, are perfect for this. (Of course, we are talking about the interview being conducted live before an audience. Variations on that—interviewing on the radio or through a webinar situation—will also be explored.) This chapter includes two important component parts that address essential interviewing practices that must be followed by the presenter. The first of these are tips for securing an author for an interview purpose, and just as essentially, pointers on how to conduct an interview. My purpose in sharing my experiences in interviewing is to guide you away from asking standard, easy, predictable questions that are bound to bore both the writer and the audience, and steer you toward posing questions that, while not "tricky" (meaning, with the intention of confusing or embarrassing the interviewee), come at the author and his or her book from an inventive perspective that will spur the author to answer in sentences and ideas they may not have expressed in previous interviews. That's the goal: make your interview fresh.)

Chapter 6 will cover panel discussions. A panel discussion is definitely a step upward in our plan of increased librarian involvement in book programming. The librarian organizer has a great resource available to him or her for putting together a panel discussion: the library staff. So, on this first level in panel presentation, the program organizer has pretty-much an already made program: asking a small group of your librarians who work in selection or in readers' advisory to think of, say, ten recent books added to the library collection—fiction or non-fiction or both—and prepare a brief talk about each one.

Of course, we aren't about to leave these librarians-as-panelists in the lurch. In this chapter I will suggest what to include in a brief "chat" about a book. If you have four librarians willing to participate in public speaking—specifically, in this case, sitting on a panel before an audience of—whoever the librarian wants to be the audience. The public—yes, of course; which usually means an evening program. Other librarians in your library or in the library system? Absolutely. This is an excellent way of keeping librarians aware of what's being added to the library shelves they may not be aware of. Librarians from outside your system, representing librarians not just like you (say you're a public librarian, then do a program like this for school librarians in your area, which means, of course, a couple YA librarians would be great for your panel to discuss books pushed for adults in this age group or to present titles that are published for adults but are very suitable for a YA readership).

This kind of panel can, of course, be employed on a monthly basis when branch librarians come to a central meeting place and a large part of the reason for this monthly convocation is to inform the branches what new books will or have been added to the main library collection, now available or soon to be available for borrowing by branch patrons.

The next level of panel is also suited to interlibrary purposes for all staff (including interested tech and shelf people) as well as the general public (a lunchtime program would be the perfect setting; regularly scheduled so the program develops a consistent following). The panelists—and I should state here that to call itself a "panel," a panel needs to be comprised of at least three speakers. One or two individuals can only be referred to simply as "speakers"—are charged with giving thumbnail analysis—plot summary and critical comments, all in capsule format—to, say, five to six books that rank as favorites of theirs. These can be as loosely presented as just "favorite books," or "favorite novels" or "favorite non-fiction books," or as tightly presented as favorite mystery novels or other fiction genres; or favorite historical novels, or every other fiction genre; or favorite non-fiction adventure stories; or favorite picture books for pre-readers, or YA novels sure to interest boys. The possibilities are endless, and the decision on a theme is up to the organizer—in consultation with other staff members, of course. And also suggested—I'd say required—is that at least half the program should be about books for youth and the panel include, as I spoke about above, librarians involved in youth work.

Author readings are one thing—one thing to get involved in, and will present itself as moderately involving—but having an author come to the library to speak is another thing, the subject of chapter 4. In the first place—for the first time in our exploration of the levels of librarian participation in book and author programs in the library—this kind of situation may involve money. How much money depends on who the author is. If you desire Hillary Clinton to come speak at your library, your pockets better be very deep; on the other hand, a local author with, say, two published novels to his or her credit but not a huge name behind him or her, can indeed present an engaging program. The difference between Hillary Clinton and a not-well-known author will mean a difference in publicity, and this chapter will explain the differences. An author program in which a single author talks about his or her writing experiences—you tell him what to talk about—has "rules" to live by, and I will discuss these in this chapter as well. And the guiding principle I suggest will also include presenting a two-author or multiauthor program.

Let me remind the reader that in all the above-cited book-and-author situations, I will also see the program through the eyes of the organizing librarian who will also be performing as the moderator of the presentation; for which, in each case, in each chapter, I will provide guidelines for the moderating process.

What could turn out to be an interesting and even quite popular program is a panel consisting of readers drawn from your pool of library patrons who are comfortable with discussing new or favorite books they have been reading. This kind of program offers peculiar challenges, but at the same time some distinctive rewards, which I will analyze in chapter 6. This kind of program, intended primarily for the public rather than library staff (who, of course, would be advised to attend, for the sake of what they could learn about the reading interests and tastes of their community: lessons, in readers' advisory, in other words), would require lots of advance preparation; thus, doing it on a regular basis may limit the time between programs. The nature of, and the necessary steps in, organizing and presenting a program of this nature will be discussed in chapter 6.

Chapter 7 presents details about sponsoring writer-in-residence programs and organizing and presenting an annual book award. These two types of programs are great library attention-getters. In its full fledge, the annual book award is presented in-person to the author (which means cash and a medal of some sort), who has agreed long in advance to come to town (which is a very important point; giving the author the award is contingent upon him or her agreeing to show up) for a banquet that will celebrate the award.

Even more intense and labor-intensive program—in fact, a major undertaking—will be addressed in chapter 8. This type of program, tried in many communities and usually quite successful, is called by different names and titles, but primarily it is the one-book, one-city idea. Regardless of the label the program is given, all one-book, one-city programs have the same basic premise, which is to draw a community together by way of reading and discussing the same book; and, as an important auxiliary purpose, to promote literacy. History tells us that the idea originated with Nancy Pearl, who was at the time the Director of the Washington (State) Center for the Book; but reiterations of Nancy's original program have proliferated across the country. And let me restate the point I broached in the first sentence of this paragraph: this is a big, big undertaking involving lots of people. In fact, it pretty much involves the whole community. Obviously, then, it is not a program to be taken lightly, to be embarked upon thinking that you as the program supervisor can do it all on your own.

Who decides what book to choose, and the criteria for selecting a community-wide read will be discussed. Promotion is paramount for the success of this kind of program, and promotional strategies will be discussed. Essentially, then, the thrust of this chapter is all the events that can lead, that can be derived from, one community involved in reading one book.

My bottom-line suggestion at this point is, jump into the world of book and author programs and have a great time doing it. Hopefully, my words to come will ensure that.

Chapter One

Let's Talk about Basic Public Speaking

Librarians who are involved with book programs and author events realize they aren't always the "talent" on stage on such occasions—meaning, they often function as the help that smooths the path of the author who is being featured or are the vehicle whereby information and opinions about books are shared and are not necessarily themselves the center of attention. But let's not dismiss the important role the librarian plays in these programs and events, which is, after all, the "meat" of this book: that is, the importance of the librarian's role.

Why We Should Care about Public Speaking

Librarians, as we shall observe as the chapters of this book unfold, are at the center of it all, and are the glue that holds the programs and events together. But more than that, the various situations and occasions and events we will analyze in forthcoming chapters often call for the librarian, as event introducer, program moderator, or sole speaker, to exhibit skills in public speaking.

Yes, your audience will flock to your facility to hear Jonathan Franzen read from his latest book, but the tone—the professional tone you seek—of the occasion is launched and set by you the introducer. Awkward, bashful, inarticulate opening comments will put the audience on edge, embarrass the author, and may cause the event to be remembered by the audience in less-than-glowing terms.

And if the librarian is conducting live interviews with an author, or is giving book chats to fellow librarians, or moderating a panel of authors requiring extensive interchange between the librarian-moderator and the panel authors, the librarian's public speaking skills are even more on display.

Old Adages

An old maxim floats widely in the land, addressing the common fear of public speaking. It says that to rid yourself of the dread of public speaking—to at least lessen your nerves to a substantial degree—you should imagine your audience sitting before you in their underwear! As the thinking behind the saying has it, seeing your audience half-naked in your mind's eye is supposed to reduce their intimidation factor. In their skivvies, they are next to harmless, leaving you as speaker with the upper hand.

You laugh! I laugh, too. I laugh because I can't imagine it working. You have the upper hand regardless of the state of dress or undress of your audience. The room is yours to command. Everyone is there to hear *you*. As a college professor once told a class I was in, "No, this is not a discussion class. There is one person in the room who knows the information to be covered and everyone else is here to learn that information."

Trying to picture all those people in their underwear—in your mind's eye, of course—is simply, in my book, too much unnecessary mental work, too much mental distraction at a moment when you certainly do not need to be distracted from the task at hand, which is, of course, delivering your public performance. *Focusing* is of the utmost importance right now, and this whole underwear nonsense only threatens to shift your focus from what it should be on.

The second maxim you often hear is that most people would rather have a root canal than speak in public! I've heard this so many times over the years that it has become, to my ears, a cliché. To someone who has never had a root canal, having one sounds pretty horrible to contemplate, especially if you know exactly what the dentist is doing.

Let me say this: I have had seven root canals and not one has been painful. Time-consuming, yes, but not painful. And let me further risk antagonizing you: I love public speaking. I know I'm good at it, and we all tend to enjoy the things we are good at.

The primary issue for us to address in this chapter is the problem of settling one's nerves before and during public speaking. A speaker so nervous that cotton-mouth is causing near-choking on dry words from a nearly closed throat is so awfully painful to watch and hear. The audience stays fixated on the speaker's nervousness—which, besides choking on dry words, includes the look of discomfort and often fear so obviously indicated by darting eyes, and often an obsessive attention to necklace or tie or glasses. It becomes a struggle for the audience to focus on the speaker's points and ideas and opinions.

Of course, we've all witnessed public speakers who, after a couple minutes into their presentation, calm down and smooth out, seeing that there really is nothing hostile about the speaker-audience partnership. I suppose that in business presentations, what the speaker has to say, if she or he is, say, a CEO and CFO, will not always be received well and may turn an anxious audience into an angry one. But in this book we're dealing with the world of authors and books and book lovers, where the sharing of ideas is customarily exciting rather than offensive. If your speakers turn out to be offensive or otherwise inappropriate—well, that's an issue we will take up in a later chapter.

Yet even the speakers who are able to execute a five-minute turnaround from being nearly catatonic with fear to being reasonably relaxed may never reach a point where they project confidence and a complete lack of nervousness. There may always be a strain in the voice.

Gaining Experience

So, my first—not actually piece of advice per se—*observation* about public speaking is this: gain *experience* in doing so. That may sound like a lame, plain, nontherapeutic remedy. True, it's not actually a remedy, in terms of a painkiller that can rather quickly rid you of a headache. It won't help you if you've been called on to perform a one-time-only speaking engagement and the event is close at hand. If the thought of what you're facing, over your probable objections, strikes terror in your heart, then you undoubtedly have no thoughts of gaining further experience. "Just this one time," you say. "Let's get this horror over with—and never again will I be dragged into doing something like this." But I say wait and see. That actual public speaking experience may turn out to be not so bad, and perhaps it will even be enjoyable. You may decide not to dismiss any future engagements, and you may even want to explore future opportunities.

If organizing and presenting book and author programs are an aspect of your job, or will become an aspect of your new or rewritten job, or if you have the idea you'd like to volunteer to be the book-and-author programming person in the absence of someone whose actual job description includes the coordination of such programs, then you have the opportunity to gain *experience*. With the accrual of experience, you can move past any discomfort level to a level of handling public speaking that is relaxed, and that will strike your audience as if you were conducting a private conversation with a person (such as a book author) you've known for a long time and with whom you feel comfortable around.

Every occasion will instill in you an increased level of confidence. You will take from each occasion a mental history of what you did well and what you still need to work on and polish further, and such a consciousness in that direction will in time reduce the list of "needs work" items and lengthen the list of "look what I do well" items.

But, if you are stepping into a public library role that has as one of its significant responsibilites an increasing involvement in book and author programs, and you really have little experience under your belt, I have a suggestion for the short term, something you can do right now that will increase your confidence level away from the judgmental eyes of your cohorts: *Join a book club*. And join one that has no association or affiliation with your library. *Join right away.* Learn the title of the next book they will be discussing, and show up and participate. Don't expect to dominate; you don't even *want* to dominate. Add your comments, but just as importantly, listen to what the others have to say about the book under discussion. The important thing is to contribute your two cents, and maybe at the next meeting add your *six* cents, and chances are that you will rapidly arrive at a comfort level for speaking before your eight or twelve book-club cohorts, and you will realize your voice is secure and your ideas are worth paying attention to.

Gaining Confidence

These are precious beginning steps for obtaining the all-important quality of confidence. It boils down to this equation: experience equals confidence. And why is that a truth, not only in public speaking but also in so many other aspects of one's efforts in achieving a successful life? (How one defines "success" is up to the individual; for our purposes, of course, success means an effective exercise of speaking in public.) It is a truth because, in the context in which we are working here (that is, public speaking), that by standing before a group of people in a book-and-author situation on more than one occasion, you will come to trust that people who come to book programs are there, generally speaking, to feed their need to be surrounded by fellow book lovers and hear personal details about the lives and works of authors. That translates as a respectful audience eager to learn whatever you—or your panelists, as is usually the case—have to say.

Yes, there will always be one or two individuals in the audience who are there to prove they know more than you or the panel you are a part of about the subject at hand—and more about the books discussed than the authors who wrote them!—and pretty much more about everything than anyone else in the room. I say this to that: let him or her have his or her say—within a reasonable time limit—and then in a polite but firm voice, make it clear that the program must continue in a timely fashion and unfortunately there isn't sufficient time built into it for everyone to air everything they would like to express. You're sorry about that, you say. (Not really, of course, but you say so anyway.)

I promise you that the more you observe the lack of indifference or even edginess from an audience, the more your self-assurance will grow. I feel that the origin of the before-a-crowd nervousness is essentially based on the rather paranoid attitude that people are looking for your mistakes, for your hesitations, for your signs of nervousness, for you to actually stumble and break down into tears or even flee the stage. Of course you're not about to! Now, I don't subscribe to the notion—promoted in speaking guides and tutorials—that the audience is actually rooting for you. What they are expecting is for you to be calm, cool, and collected; and for you to make it easy for them to "get their money's worth" (even if they paid nothing to attend your event). So, why would they want to see a nervous breakdown in front of them?

Reading the Audience

No, I maintain that audiences are generally neutral. (Except, of course, if they are present to listen to a political figure, but what I'm talking about here is you as a public speaker and what you can expect from an audience.) That being the case, it is just as easy to please them as displease them. Remember that. Audiences can tip in either direction, so your "job" is to lead them down the yellow brick road to enjoying themselves and hearing an edifying program. How will you know if they are experiencing enjoyment with you as a speaker? Once again, experience will tell you—no, I will go out on a limb here and say that even the first time you are in front of an audience, you will pick up on the "vibe" coming in your direction. All audiences give off a vibe. It may be mixed; the rapt attention of the absorbed audience member mixed with seat-shifting of the less drawn-in. But the predominant vibe—and there will always be one—will send a stronger airwave message to the speaker; and, as I've said, audiences are generally supportive, so the sense you are eliciting from them will inform you of the program's success—of the audience's approval of what you are saying—and you will take that good vibe immediately to heart, and as your presentation develops, your confidence in yourself and what you've chosen to be the subject of your talk will grow exponentially. I've seen it happen; we've all seen it happen. A speaker tense at the beginning of the presentation melts into relaxation as the minutes pass, as the speaker realizes she (or he) truly does know what she (or he) is talking about, which is in turn being recognized by an accepting audience.

And you know as well as I do that this is a sight with which to connect audience to speaker; and, too, that the speaker's early moments of nervousness are easily and quickly forgotten, wiped away by the speaker's gained poise, which is how he or she will be recalled. "Oh, yes, he was a good speaker," will be what the audience members say to each other as they file out of the room; and will be how the audience members think about the speaker at later times, when the program is remembered and spoken about.

Improving Your Voice

Let's talk about your voice. If the group you are addressing is of a size where you have to raise your voice to be heard—meaning, more than a dozen to fifteen individuals in your audience—you will probably be—you should be—amplified by a microphone. Speaking into a microphone isn't necessarily instinctive; most speakers need some polishing before they can successfully use one. (Even in this aspect of public speaking, we still come back to the old bugga-boo called "experience.") Here are some points about "mike speaking" that may give you "instant" experience:

1. Don't lean into and away from the microphone. You don't want your voice to constantly increase and decrease in volume. You don't want the audience to strain to hear you one minute and then nearly need to cover their ears the next. And there is nothing more irritating for an audience than to hear the boom and crackle of a speaker's mike when lips are practically right on it. If you are speaking from a podium with a smallish mike on a thin stem, adjust it quickly to your height and maintain your posture. You'll soon realize—the audience will tell you (literally!)—if you are being heard in the back. If not, increase the volume of your voice a small degree—don't start shouting, of course—but don't, as I've said, interrupt your erect posture to lean in close to the mike. Slouching is not good; we were all done with that when we left college and thought professors who propped themselves up on the podium were "cool." Slouching is not cool in grown-up public speaking.

2. At the risk of sounding sexist, I will proceed to say what I feel I have to say at this point. If you are a female speaker and you recognize the fact that your voice is high-pitched, understand the mike's tendency to elevate the pitch; and nervousness, unfortunately, has the same effect. I am not suggesting a fake-pseudo-Tallulah Bankhead (FYI: an American movie and stage star of the 1930s and 1940s, well-known for her deep, "sexy" voice, like someone with bronchitis) voice be adopted; what I am saying is that if you can, and can keep it consistent, please speak in the lower register of your voice. Let's face it, a high-pitched presentation has the effect of reducing the effectiveness of your words and ideas.

Know Your Material

Let's return to a topic I previously touched upon. And that's you being the authority in the room, on the occasion of you standing before an audience to deliver words you want them to hear. And everyone else is there to learn the knowledge behind these words and absorb the experience behind the knowledge. A cohort of mine—a well-respected figure in the library world, the very mention of whose name causes librarians to recognize that individual's contribution and high professional position—and I were discussing another figure in the library world, who'd just been appointed to an important ALA committee; but her name hardly evokes warm feelings. As it turns out, several years ago the latter had been invited to a local public library system to give a lecture on a certain aspect of public library work; my cohort, who was employed at the time in a large suburban library system, of course chose to go downtown to this woman's program, to take advantage of this potentially informative evening; she went en masse with other suburban librarians in her area who were well-grounded in the aspect of librarianship that this woman would be talking about. They were leaders in the field, as a matter of fact.

The guest librarian—the subject of my friend's and my conversation—came swaggering in and talked down to her audience, apparently trying to convince them of her authority simply through her "authoritative" (read "arrogant") attitude and not by her command of the subject. And it became clear she didn't know what she was talking about, particularly to this group of suburban librarians already deeply involved in this aspect of contemporary librarianship, and the Q and A session afterward confirmed to them in no uncertain terms that she was inadequate to the task set before her.

Know your material. If you're asked to speak on a subject you are not well versed in, you have two choices: decline the invitation, or use the time between being invited and the date for delivering your talk to learn all you can about the subject at hand. Regardless of your previous newness to the material, either know it or don't go stand before an audience to talk about it. Familiarity with the material will be obvious from the speaker's first uttered sentence; the confidence that familiarity brings to the speaker will be built into the words spoken and, more obviously, in the tone in which those words are couched. Or, to view the situation from the opposite angle, an absence of familiarity with the material will cast a shadow over the speaker's words and demeanor from the start. The audience will be offered the alternatives of losing interest or challenging the speaker at the program's end (hopefully at the end and not in the form of a rude and embarrassing interruption in the course of the program).

Take Your Time

One of the basic tenets of any self-help program—or self-affirmation, if you will, or even self-improvement—is encouragement to push beyond one's comfort zone in all aspects of personal endeavor, including jobs, relationships, or traveling the world. Challenge yourself, goes the admonition; take on projects, assignments, duties, or wish-fulfillments that will test your mettle and will inevitably garner you great personal satisfaction. Broadcast yourself, prove yourself, assert yourself. Don't settle for continuing to live in the nest you've created for yourself.

But I issue a warning. Exhibiting bravado sounds all well and good when asking for a raise, climbing Mount Everest, or even enrolling in a watercolor class. But tread lightly in following this advice when it comes to public speaking. If you believe you need to build up your confidence in speaking in front of an audience, think about it first before volunteering to be the *sole* speaker at a program that is intended to last for a half hour or full hour. I'm certainly not insisting that you can't do it. What I *am* saying is that if heretofore the idea of public speaking caused you to break out in a cold sweat and think of the root canal comparison, then perhaps you should forego the sole-speaker assignment for the time being and choose a path of incremental participation and difficulty, like wading into the shallow end of a pool and progressing, not necessarily slowly but at least methodically to the deep end, which usually means, in the context in which we are speaking, trying yourself out as a panel member first.

A potential speaker may not quake at the idea of carrying a whole speaking program on his or her shoulders and consequently feel perfectly adequate to volunteering to speak on a topic new to him or her. Again, I mean this: Don't jump into the deep end of the pool; begin with easier participation in which you contribute a small amount to the speaking program, and in turn you will listen to the other speakers on that topic as if they are reading sacred text. You need to learn from them, and keep educating yourself on the topic as you take on increasingly involved speaking roles, at the same time broadening and deepening your knowledge of that subject. A beginning might be simply introducing a speaker or a panel of speakers who will address the topic, as your knowledge of it can still be in the minimal or novice stage.

I would say that if you are interested in public speaking—and doing so on more than a onetime, isolated basis—becoming an acknowledged authority on some subject or other and focusing your speaking efforts within that subject framework would be a worthwhile project. If you are a librarian and are engaged in a particular task facing librarians—not full time, necessarily, but as a significant portion of your professional time—you have a ready-made subject in which to specialize and thus for extending yourself as an expert, and can offer yourself as a speaker on that subject. For instance, weeding. My cohort, Rebecca Vnuk, Adults Books Editor, Collection Management and Library Outreach here at *Booklist*, gives workshops and webinars on the subject of weeding. And, for the record, weeding is a controversial issue in the library world. Which books should go and which books should stay? How do you decide? That's why it's a controversial issue.

My point in citing Rebecca and her weeding expertise is that she took advantage of the experience—and the expertise of a mentor—available to her and built up an expertise for herself, which she has turned into a public speaking forum—namely, workshops and webinars. I know for a fact, knowing Rebecca as I do, that in her presentation mien, she projects both authority and comfort with the subject at hand and the act of public speaking. And comfort with *being* an authority.

That last point I made might raise an eyebrow. What is the difference between being comfortable with a subject and comfortable with *being* an authority on the subject? Let's say, first, that you should aspire to be *both*. Being comfortable with a subject means you know it in most of its depth and in most of the width. Enough to carry on an intelligent, informed conversation from different angles and approaches to the subject. Sufficiently informed to be a public speaker on the subject. And being comfortable with being an authority on the subject. Without boastfulness, you stand erect—literally and metaphorically—before an audience and show yourself to be the commander of your material as you know yourself to be. You know in your heart and brain that you know the material, and that is a direct link to building the confidence so required to be a good public speaker. You don't resort to arrogance to establish recognition of your authority, but neither do you demure and project an embarrassment that with your authority you are singled out and consequently to be shied away from. Nonsense! Just plain nonsense. Both get over yourself and assert yourself. The balance is a good human being and a good public speaker.

Let me end this particular discussion with this admonishment. Don't pretend to know the material. You *will* be seen through.

Typed Script or Off the Cuff?

What I have to say next will also raise some eyebrows and even hackles. Essentially, the issue I am set to address is what does a good speaker take to the podium with her or him, or, if part of a panel that remains seated while each one is taking a "turn," what do you have in front of you on the dais?

Certainly, I'm not referring to props. (If props are part of your presentation, that is another story; we're concerned here with what you are speaking from, notes or free-form). I see basically three options for what speakers use to anchor their presentation: One, a completely extemporaneous presentation, with no notes or text, just "winging it," as they say. Two, having in front of you some written notes that keep the points about the topic at hand so that none is forgotten, but fleshing out these points is done extemporaneously, drawing on what you have rehearsed to say. Three, reading from a typed script.

Here is where the contentiousness of my ideas about how much preparation is required and the best preparation method comes into play. I believe that the best technique is reading from a typed, prepared text. There, I've said it, and let the arguments begin.

It is, I believe, pretty much accepted as a universal truth that writing one's ideas down is the best way to organize and present them. The relatively slow act of putting one word on paper, then another one (or, to be more contemporary, onto the computer screen), allows a brief but important editorial oversight that speaking alone simply cannot provide. In throwing out word after word in extemporaneous mode, no matter how rehearsed the presentation has been, your mind will often bring something up out of its subconscious and you will deliver a word that is not the word you would have preferred, but just the most pragmatic one for the moment, and your sentence may emerge in a less-than-appropriate structure, with dangling modifiers and subject and verb disagreements that you know better than to fall into.

In truth, we cannot speak perfectly without a script or memorization, particularly with a bit of nerves gnawing at us. And I insist to myself that when delivering a presentation, I speak perfectly; the structure of every sentence must be immaculate and every word choice well thought out, in order to express myself in the exact vocabulary I wish it to be. In most instances—no, I'd say in *all* cases—when called upon to speaking publicly, other than something brief like introducing someone and the introduction is needed to be only a minute or two long, you are expected to sound precise and professional. Not "conversational," which is simply another term for rambling, disjointed, and hit-or-miss when coming to make the point of the speech. Not "intimate," which means substituting charm for rehearsal, not attempting to sound like you are in a conversation with only a half-dozen people at a cocktail party, holding forth on some topic or other. But an articulate possessor of important knowledge you need and want to share with your audience in a fashion that best expresses the tenets of that knowledge.

Yes, of course, there is the problem of "racing"—speeding—through your text. That would be the counterargument to reading from a prepared text. We've all heard it: prepared comments by an anxious speaker who gallops through his or her "speech" as if sitting astride a horse hell-bent on getting back to the barn and a nice oats dinner. That speech is over in half the time allotted to it in the program and probably half the time of when it was being rehearsed. The answer is, obviously, rehearse; and rehearse not just with an eye to modulation and pacing, and rising and falling emphasis, too, but also, concomitant with all that, an awareness of your tempo or speed. Read the speech aloud many times while paying close, close attention to how rapidly you are reading. Whatever, in rehearsal, you feel is an appropriately slow speed, slow it down even more. Perhaps cut the speed by an additional fraction. The audience will appreciate a careful enunciation of every word; they want, deserve, and will readily and very obviously accept the ability to understand every word from your mouth.

In fact, I make it a practice to type, in big bold letters, SLOW DOWN, at a break every two or three paragraphs in my prepared text, and to surround those words with lots of white space so these "signs" cannot be ignored.

Mixed Bag or Winging It

Here is another speaking scenario that rubs me the wrong way because it diverts any attention from what's being said to *how* it is being said: mixing reading from a prepared text with off-the-cuff remarks. I believe speakers who do that mean well. They intend to show that they have a connection to the audience, which they fear they will not achieve by giving a "pure" reading presentation.

I say "nonsense" to that. A well-read, well-paced, well-modulated script can establish a mutually beneficial connection between speaker and audience. (We'll speak about how in a short while.) And the main reason for this is because the well-rehearsed speaker keeps the talk on a constant wavelength—meaning, the speaker's voice maintains a constant level of assuredness, of gracefulness, if you will, of self-possession (in order to keep the audience in a comfortable state of listening and learning). The "comfort" thing is the issue about integrating off-the-cuff remarks into an otherwise written preparation, and I refer in this case to the comfort of the *audience*. One would think that the more a speaker could slip "off script" and put in some personal, tailored-to-the-occasion remarks, the easier it would to embrace.

Not so. This back-and-forth is jarring. When the speaker goes off script to talk off-the-cuff, his or her voice changes—ironically, from the relaxed voice of someone who knows exactly what words are to follow, and who has rehearsed those words sufficiently so that their delivery is smooth and even, to a less-secure, nervous-elevated voice, and with a look on the speaker's face saying, I'm now on thinner ice than I was. Then after a few "loose" sentences, back to the script, and chances are the speaker will hit the runway, as if it were, at a speed that is too rapid so that it will take a while to reestablish even, easily understood pacing.

Completely Ad-Libbed

The speaker who steps up to the podium with neither script nor notes is a confident speaker, relaxed before a crowd, in full possession of what he or she intends to speak about. Or *should* be, anyway. A speaker who does not meet those requirements but nevertheless wants to embark on the open seas of public speaking without—to continue the metaphor—charts and radar or even basic channel markers is a brave person. Truthfully, not *brave* at all. *Foolish* is more like it. You can bet this speaker's presentation will go many minutes over the allotted time; it's nearly a given that a noteless speaker will ramble, will stray from the topic, will bring into the talk details and explanations and asides that are exactly *that*: beside the point, that is. Unless the speaker is consistently hilarious, the audience will grow inattentive and restless. (And a speaker who is hilarious from start to finish is not common, and even if the speaker is funny, in this speculative universe, he or she will undoubtedly consume more of the allotted time.)

The prospective speaker may choose this method because it means—seems to suggest, anyway—that no preparation is necessary, and many individuals agree to speak in public with the thought that they will plan what to talk about when they step up to speak. "It will come to me. Plus, I want to be 'conversational,' not like I'm delivering a lecture." So goes their thinking. But the truth is, what you gain in time and energy in having to think in advance of the event by *not* spending extensive preparation time, you will, by a law of nature, lose in discomfort when standing before your audience with your "pants down," as it were.

So, I come around to my original position: the best public speaking scenario is reading—carefully, with slow pacing, and frequently looking up at the audience—from a prepared script. The choice is yours, of course, but I feel an urge to weigh in. And there it is.

Gaining Experience and Authority

An interview with **Rebecca Vnuk,** Adult Books Editor, Collection Management and Library Outreach at *Booklist*.

Can you tell us how you gained experience in the area of weeding library collections?

Funny story. I actually owe my passion for weeding to a Chicago alderman, Gene Schulter. Previous to my interaction with Alderman Schulter, I looked at weeding as nothing but a simple task. In 2002, while working for the Chicago Public Library, Schulter had been mistakenly led to believe that library weeding was nothing more than the mass destruction of library materials, with no thought process involved. He literally stormed my workspace one day, threatening to have me fired for weeding books. It was then that I realized that weeding was not only necessary but also polarizing. My previous weeding experience had been a relatively easy part of my regular job duties at the first small public library I worked for.

This particular project, which was quite contentious with both the public and some of the staff, was a huge undertaking and took many months. It gave me a real respect for the task of weeding and a close understanding of how to approach and execute a project. My next two weeding projects were far less dramatic but were just as large—one involved weeding nearly ten thousand books from the fiction section of a library that was gearing up for a move; the next involved weeding nearly half of the entire adult collection for a library that was in desperate need of an overhaul—and luckily, the project had the library board's full backing of a doubled book budget for replacements.

Use Humor—But Be Careful

Unless you are a stand-up comedian, your presentation should not be a series of one-liners, shaggy-dog stories, and anecdotes that you the speaker believes are hilarious. My feeling about humor is this: one, at most two, humorous moments is sufficient in a public speaking event. Any more than that, and your presentation risks coming off as reaching and stretching. That leaves the audience uncomfortable. No one wants to see the underpinnings of a program, to observe the speaker straining for effect. Contrary to what many people believe, I say don't lead off your presentation with a joke. Perhaps maybe one line of soft humor, but then quickly get into the "serious" talk you have been contracted for. It's been my experience that one good line of something humorous a third of the way through the speech, or even at the halfway point, will mark the speech in the audience's consciousness/memory as "and he was funny, too!" That's what you want: your talk to be serious and helpful and address the issues at hand, but doggone it, you were "funny, too!"

Chocolate

What? What does chocolate have to do with public speaking, or anything to do with what we've been discussing, for that matter?

If you are the sole speaker or the person who organized a program of one speaker or a panel of more than one speaker, then "work the crowd." I have observed renowned librarian Joyce Saricks do this by greeting the audience at the door with a basket of chocolate kisses, which she also takes with her as she walks among the seated audience asking if she missed anyone or if someone would like a second piece. The effect is palpable: the audience sits back and enjoys the candy or enjoys watching other people doing so, and it is immediately under the spell of the speakers, having been made to feel that they, as individuals, are welcome and appreciated for their attendance.

Basically, the speaker or speakers have won the audience over even before the program has begun. When it comes to chocolate, we're all besties!

Chapter Two

Book Clubs, Part I

THE BASICS

Let us first define our terms. In this chapter, in this book as a whole, I consider the term "book club" to be synonymous with "reading group." Just so you know at the outset, I mean the same thing by those two expressions. As a matter of fact, a third term exists, which combines the two: "reading club." But I will not use this third one. If you've encountered it elsewhere, feel safe in assuming that it means nothing different than "book club" or "reading group."

History of Book Clubs

By any definition of the term, book discussion groups do not present a new cultural trend. In various incarnations and venues, groups of readers have gathered regularly to hear interesting books being discussed. For instance, Prairie Avenue on the near South Side of Chicago is where the moneyed elite in the 1890s built their unrestrained domiciles. Prairie Avenue, in fact, was understood to be "the sunny street that held the sifted few." Of course, this being post-Great Fire Chicago, the "moneyed elite" meant the great industrialists who were contributing to driving Chicago to great economic and population heights for it to become the second largest city in the country after New York City. One such industrialist who resided on Prairie Avenue was one John J. Glessner, who was high up at International Harvester and whose Prairie Avenue house exhibited a unique design by the noted and respected architect Henry Hobson Richardson.

The novelist Arthur Meeker, popular in the 1930s and 1940s, wrote an informative memoir of growing up on Prairie Avenue during the street's heyday as a center of high society, called *Chicago with Love*. He mentions the Glessner House and the Glessner family in the following context: Mrs. Glessner founded and maintained what she called the Monday Morning Reading Club. (There is that term again.) Being a patroness of the arts apparently was a cap she proudly wore, and her Reading Club stood as manifestation of her artistic pursuits.

The rules were these: the group met every two weeks for two hours, from October to May. The women sewed while listening to a professional reader. To become a member required an invitation. Photographs exist of the assembled Reading Club members, and one of these photographs appears on the Glessner House website (Glessner House is a museum these days, the house and all its contents having been willed by Mrs. Glessner to the American Institute of Architects) that shows the ladies of the club gathered on the outdoor steps of the house one fine day. *All women*, of course, which was in keeping with the custom of the times in which the group flourished. (It suffered disbandment in 1930, when the ill Mrs. Glessner could no longer maintain the club.)

Women Only?

That seems to have been the universal case. Early book groups consisted pretty much exclusively of women. Did they automatically close their doors to their husbands, or was the predominantly female makeup (no pun intended!) the result of women—back then, as now—being more avid readers than men, and, perhaps due to this factor as well: unlike today, women stayed home to attend to family matters while their husbands participated in the workforce, thus the woman could slip out for "book clubbing."

These factors were certainly borne out a little closer to my home and life than elegant, exclusive Prairie Avenue in Chicago. I come from a medium-sized, working-class town by the name of Mattoon, located in flat, flat, central Illinois. But my hometown has a distinction: it is the seat of the Mattoon Women's Reading Club. The MWRC has been going strong—uninterruptedly—since 1877, making it *the longest-running women's book group in Illinois!*

My parents socialized with Mr. and Mrs. Clawson, he the principal of Mattoon High School. The Clawsons and my family often took fishing vacations together, during which Mrs. Clawson and my mother would spend *their* time sitting outside in the shade reading. (I alternated between fishing and reading.) I remember that on more than one occasion Mrs. Clawson mentioned she would be giving a presentation on the book she was engaged in to her reading club. Little did I know at the time her reading club was none other than the venerable Mattoon Women's Reading Club.

Reading is taken seriously by the Mattoon Women's Reading Club members; they take pride in *not* being a social club. In fact, according to the bylaws, refreshments are not allowed at meetings, nor have they *ever* been permitted. The club meets twice a month, with one member giving a presentation on a book she has just read. That's a format that is found in various book clubs over the land, and it is this particular format that we will look closer at later in this chapter.

A very contemporary take on women being the predominant demographic in book clubs can be found in the book *Reading Lolita in Tehran: A Memoir in Books,* by Azar Nafisi, published in 2008. The common conception of a reading club is to experience a good time: "good" defined in this context as relaxed, informative, and sustaining conversation about books in an open setting *not* under the cover of darkness.

But Azar Nafisi tells a different story. For two years every Tuesday night, in Iran's capital, she, a teacher, met with a small, select group of her female students to read Western classics actually *forbidden* to be read in the Islamic state. An important theme about book clubs emerges: serious book clubs are serious because their members are serious readers who, simply put, *have* to read.

Apparently, female domination of book clubs arises naturally from a circumstance that sparked the emergence of book discussion groups in the first place. It is common knowledge that in the eighteenth and nineteenth centuries, women were at least discouraged, if not outright being denied the opportunity, from getting an education. Sewing and watercolor painting were sufficient. But those centuries saw an increase in the number and intent of women who had the means as well as the leisure time to gather in each other's drawing rooms on a regular basis and listen to or discuss authors and books, as a form of self-education, in an attempt to lessen the distance between male education and their own.

Thus was born the reading group as we know it, an intellectual "watering hole" for the woman who wanted to cultivate her mind but could find no shelter and solace within traditional educational systems. Could this explain, too, why the majority of library borrowers, to this day, are females? Bottom line is that usage came to be viewed as a female activity—and, unfortunately, still is.

Librarian Involvement in Book Clubs

In as natural a relationship as exists anywhere under the sun, book clubs are closely involved with libraries and librarians. It doesn't take a rocket scientist to see a commonality between the two. There is no better authority on reading than a librarian; no better general authority on books that a wide range of general readers would be interested in. Having been a full-time reviewer and then an editor at *Booklist*, I pride myself on my vast book knowledge (of nonacademic books, of course, those about which we speak), but, on the other hand, every time I attend a conference of librarians or give a book program to an audience of librarians, I am struck anew by the wide and deep resource every librarian represents in his or her knowledge of a whole "library" of books they carry around in their head. It follows that they love to discuss the books they know—either love or passionately dislike, but most commonly the former—and to encourage other people to discuss books in any context.

This "axis of love" is the basis of librarians' interest and involvement in book clubs; it's where personal and professional interests intersect and feed nourishment to each side of a librarian's mind.

Still Going Strong

How many people are involved in book clubs today? An interesting question, but it is akin to the difficult to answer, "How many stars exist in space?" It has been estimated that as late as 2011, more than five million adults are believed to be in reading groups (a figure which does not include online groups—a type that we will discuss at a later point in this chapter).[1]

But securing definite statistics on the matter is impossible; book clubs can be widely advertised and thus "registered" for public accounting, or can fly indefinitely under any sort of regulatory radar, with meetings conducted in someone's living room, specifics on when and where spread by phone, e-mail, or word of mouth, and thus all the world is none the wiser. But, doggone it, that's the way it should be. It's nobody's business but the group members' business.

However, how do you even begin to count the number of clubs in existence? Obviously, we have to rely on anecdote in the absence of cold, hard facts. I think everyone would agree that anecdotes tell us book clubs are doing fine. How many times have you heard someone say that their book club has disbanded? Rarely if ever do you hear that. The person you are talking to might have dropped out of a club or neglected to attend for a long period of time, but the club having evaporated into thin air? Does it happen? Scant evidence—anecdotal—exists to support it happening frequently. As we have seen, the book discussion concept has been around for a long time and there is no indication of its current popularity abating. But what *has* occurred is an *evolution* of book clubs.

Evolutionary Changes

A term to remember when it comes to learning about how book clubs have evolved over the years since the Monday Morning Reading Club of Prairie Avenue in Chicago is "niche." The classic definition of niche is, of course, a recess in a wall, especially for a statue. The more contemporary usage is a place—more figurative these days than literal—one occupies in society, at work, within the family where you are at home and know your surroundings comfortably. With regard to book groups, what is meant by "niche" is gearing the club being formed to read and discuss one kind of book, which may be a certain genre of fiction or a specific topic of nonfiction book.

Let's return for a brief moment to the Mattoon Women's Reading Club. In the *Chicago Tribune* article that "blew the cover off" this organization—not really, since there was never anything clandestine about the membership or proceedings; the article simply brought Chicago-area attention to something culturally interesting happening in downstate Illinois—staff reporter (and author of the piece) Barbara Brotman quoted club member Eulalee Anderson (who, by the way, lived around the corner from my family and was often a substitute teacher in my high school French class) as saying, about the club's preference for nonfiction, "Fiction books are entertaining, but they don't teach you as much."[2]

So, as we see, the Mattoon Women's Reading Club practiced a "niche" selection policy for a long time, long before book clubs became ubiquitous and before anyone had the reaction that there was anything "niche-esque" about this club's partiality for nonfiction. Today, we realize and relish the fact that the specific types of books that can dominate and thus define a book club are endless. For instance, biography is an extensive and popular category; biography cuts across all nonfiction categories, from history to medical science, from writing to dancing to politics. The general focus of your club may be on "biography," but the range within that subject heading is broad. And another for instance: gay and lesbian groups have a rich field to till, if LGBT-oriented books are to exclusively form your selection lists. The Bible, too, can define a niche reading group, and that group's focus can include not only actually reading the Bible but also reading books oriented toward the Bible, such as a biography of Jesus, a history of the Jesuits, or a history of Christian holidays.

We will discuss the general characteristics of a good book-discussion book later in this chapter, as well as provide a reading list of actual book titles that have solid appeal for discussion in book-club situations.

Book-Club Formats

Not only by the types of books a book group is interested in can the group be defined, members also have options in terms of the organization and procedures involved. These days, book clubs generally are of the single-title type, wherein all members read the same book simultaneously and with each person responsible for securing a copy for themselves. Obviously, there has to be a system in place for selecting titles well in advance, so that everyone has a chance to obtain a copy and read it. What works most successfully when it comes to determining what book to read next is a rotation through the membership in a strictly adhered-to order (alphabetically, date of entry into the club, whatever), allowing the person who is next on the list to choose the title for the group (with no arguing by other club members or insistence that "I will not read *that* book"). Democracy in action; this is a fair way to decide.

In harking back to a practice in earlier book groups, contemporary book groups may elect to be a one-person-type group, which means that one person in the group reads a book on their personal time and then reports on it at a meeting, while the rest of the membership sits back and listens. (Think back to the Mattoon Women's Reading Club in my hometown.) The ways of selecting a book to be read and reported on by a single member can range from a simple method—the designated reader/discusser simply choosing a book they happen to want to talk about—to a more involved situation, by which the membership has a selection meeting once a year to put together a list of books that members have indicated an interest in reading, and at that same meeting the membership votes on which ones should make the cut.

A variation on this format is this: the book selected by an individual member is *read* to the group, while the others listen. Regular commentary by the listeners should be encouraged, and the best way to handle breaks in the flow is to have the reader stop reading at the end of each chapter or section of the book, to open up the proceedings to questions and reactions. Then the reader would continue with the next chapter. Given the length of most books, even relatively "short" books, a second meeting may be in order.

What I've described is a special kind of book club, in that people may be eager to attend at first—"It would be like listening to an audiobook"—but by the second or third meeting they've decided it's boring. At least with an audiobook, you can start and stop it at your convenience and be in comfortable surroundings and in comfortable clothing to devote maximum attention. I must say, this kind of book club is my least favorite. If your group is interested in the one-member, one-book concept, I suggest the format in which one member discusses for the group's benefit a book she or he has just read, rather than reading the book aloud to the group. Both variations, however, represent such a low participation that members—and I'm even referring to the core members who may have been heartily in favor of the format at the outset—nevertheless may grow bored.

The Rush to Lunch

This type of club I've been talking about, when only one person has the book in hand, and when it has a relatively open membership, attracts lots of people who want to feel that by attending a monthly "talk" about a book, they are dipping a toe into book culture. But, really, they experience the event as a social outing. And by "open" membership, let me give example. Several years ago, for about three or four months running, I was asked by a suburban Chicago country club to be the featured reviewer at the monthly meeting of the women's book club. One person was to read a book—*me*, or other featured reviewers—and during a late morning session, talk about the book. One had to be careful to select a book on a topic that a range of people would be interested in. (It was the old nonfiction situation at play.

To a general audience, nonfiction is easier to talk about than a novel. Most general readers don't know enough about the critical components of fiction to deliver a talk more than just a few minutes in length as a solo speaker, whereas with nonfiction, you have the subject matter at hand to share details about—and with which to fill up the time!)

I customarily had a comfortable sense that I'd chosen appropriate books for the group, which usually numbered about 50 attendees. Looking out over the audience, I would always see interested faces; and at the end of my presentation, several people would have questions. But I had to laugh every time I gave a presentation to this group; in the back row were the ladies who lunch. As soon as my remarks were finished—meaning, before any question and answer exchange could hold the audience further—the back row would stand and make a mad dash to the country club's dining room, to be seated and to get their lunch orders in before the rest of the crowd arrived. Culture was fine, but lunch ranked more important!

Book Swap

Another kind of book club that has a very interesting premise and is apparently gaining ground involves the actual swapping of a physical book among the membership—although the "membership" is usually defined as those who show up and are prepared to participate. Anyone who wants to "sponsor" a session calls a meeting, by any of social media and word of mouth, in a public space, usually a bar or coffeehouse. Instructions are these: select a book you really like, in a newer or advanced-copy format, and bring it to the event wrapped plainly with nothing written on the packaging, and by whatever round-robin method is chosen, someone opens your book and you rush to their side and extoll the virtues of your book and explain why that person can't possibly avoid the opportunity of reading it. Obviously, no one has homework to do prior to the session, yet it is a great way to discuss books and learn about new books from people you may not even know but have a connection to by way of the love of books and reading. What this type of format presents, too, is continuously adding to your personal library but at the same time "weeding" books you have thought highly of but don't really need to keep in your possession.

Book Clubs on Television and the Radio

These are customarily called "broadcast clubs." Pretty much all of us have seen or heard them, or at least run across them as we are flipping the channels or turning the radio dial. In a regularly scheduled interview format, a book critic or a broadcast journalist with demonstrated expertise in books and authors interviews authors of recently released books. The authors are usually involved as part of their publisher's promotional campaign; and it is usually the publisher—the publicity agent who is heading this particular author's media campaign—who contacts the radio or television station, offering their author to be interviewed. These programs, whether local or national, are a personally edifying way to keep up with what's new in the publishing world. The point of these programs is to get listeners to the library or bookstore to get their hands on the book. Later, we will discuss how the public librarian can play a role in these programs and as a result enhance library usage, as well as the library's reputation.

Online Book Clubs

A considerable portion of the world's business has moved online. And book clubs have moved online as well. Not all, of course, but many. (But a significant portion of book clubbers still insist that in-person, face-to-face meetings with other members is an important component of the book club experience.) It's only a natural progression in the evolution of the book club as we have been discussing. These book clubs are virtual, of course; no one is coming face-to-face with other club members in a library or a living room or a coffee shop. But the basic book club rules apply. People form an online club like they would an in-person club (how to start a club in the first place is addressed later in this chapter) or join one that is already up and running. The online book club is conducive to the niche-type of club. Readers can join all kinds of online book chats but will gravitate more readily to one that is geared to the type of book they are most interested in reading and discussing.

Presenting a Book Club

Let us now turn to an all-important topic to which all of our discussion about the history and types of book clubs had been prefatory: the librarian's role in fostering local book groups; and that role ranges, as we will see, in the degree of the librarian's participation, from simply supplying a meeting space in the library for a book group already organized and "governed" by its own procedures, to actually organizing and even leading a book club under the library's auspices. Truth be told, I employ the word "simply" inappropriately. "Simply" opening up a space in your library isn't so simple. To make opening of your library's facilities a successful experience for both the book club and the host library, some considerations need to be given thought to.

Simply put, and there *is* a simple point to it all—the first, of course, is the distinct advantage to permitting a book club to meet under your library's roof. *It brings people into the library.* And that's a goal close to the heart of every librarian. Traffic. All members of a book club will be avid readers; it goes with the territory. But not all will be active library *users.* (Although in this age of closed bookstores, unless good readers are ordering from Amazon, where are they getting their "fix" if not at the local public library?) But once the library has opened its doors to a book club, members of said club, to get to their meeting space, will probably need to step through the circulation and reference areas, where, of course, new books are displayed and other library programs are advertised. And thus we have the means and opportunity for the librarian under whose roof the club is meeting to pitch the library's resources—even if the librarian's actual role in the book club is to, basically, simply provide meeting space.

As a librarian, if having a book club in your midst is a new idea, think about your space offerings before broadcasting the availability and suitability of the library for book club usage. Basically, where would you put people? You'll have to have an enclosed meeting space; in other words, having group members sitting around a table in an open public space will be too big a noise distraction for your other library patrons as well as for the club members themselves trying to carry on a conversation. The ideal, obviously, is if your library has a conference room. The room where your library board meets, perhaps. It's a relatively secluded, isolated space, in terms of soundproofing.

If your library has a large program room, one that is usually used for public and staff presentations, a book club can convene in one corner if spreading out over the whole room is impractical for the flow of good conversation. It goes without saying, but the larger your library, the more meeting space is available. But if your library is small and you really don't have a meeting space, here is something to keep in mind. I worked in my small hometown public library during summers when I was in college. The library board would meet once a month, convening in our break room, sitting around a large table in café chairs. Nothing fancy, but it worked; and I think, in retrospect, if book clubs had been common back then and my public librarian wanted to have some participating role in fostering one, opening up the break room for a couple hours once a month would have been a workable move. Basically, what I'm saying is, most any space will do, as long as it offers a degree of privacy.

Refreshments?

Speaking of my hometown library's break room leads to another consideration that the sponsoring or space-providing librarian needs to think about. What is your policy regarding refreshments in the library? Allow? Disallow? If your library generally disallows, can exceptions be made, especially for a book club? After all, chances are that when your board meets in your library, at least coffee is served, correct? If your function is strictly providing space, have a policy formulated about bringing food and beverages in before you agree to, or seek out, a book group meeting on your premises.

Speaking of roles, then, leads to a consideration of policies in general about a group using your facilities. Do you have an agreement form, with rules and regulations specified, which you will require a member of the book group to sign? At least a basic, simple agreement is advised, by which the signee agrees that the room will be left exactly as it was found; if food and beverages may be brought in, all "leftovers" will be taken from the premises and plates, etc., will be discarded (and if the privilege of refreshments is allowed, an extra trash receptacle in the room is suggested). If any kind of extra security is necessary under your library's security plan, that needs to be spelled out in the agreement (as well as any fees involved in the providing of extra security); and anything else that past experiences in providing meeting space for non-staffers has informed you is important and needs to be addressed in the written agreement. It's like a prenup. It's for "just in case."

Of course, the hosting librarian will need to learn from the book group leader or someone in the group who is representing that group as a whole, upon coming to an agreement that you will be providing space in your library for the group, if this is a onetime situation or to be a regularly scheduled event. Most likely the latter, but the hosting librarian will want to encourage the group to meet on a regular basis—meaning, the first Tuesday of every month, the fifteenth of every month, etc. This will eliminate lots of confusion on the librarian's part as to reserving the space at times when there is no conflict with another book group or even staff meetings, board meetings, and, if you are using the break room, staff breaks! Make certain that whoever on your staff is responsible for reserving various spaces in the library for various events, that care is taken that conflicting dates never occur. Obviously, that would result in bad public relations, and the major purpose of hosting a book club in your midst is to extend to the public only *good* relations with the library.

Good Public Relations

A question to ask the group leader or the member who is speaking for the group, is whether they want any publicity. Closed membership, which characterizes most traditional book clubs ("closed" in that new members can join if they talk to members beforehand but "closed" in that the doors are not open to members of the public who just show up and hope to get in on the discussion), is the kind that will be interested in using library space and, generally speaking, need no advertising of upcoming meetings. But for the good of the library—again, thinking in terms of public relations and letting the public know how busy and relevant the public library is to the life of the community—it would be worth asking if the book club meetings can be posted on the library website as "upcoming events," with some mention that the meetings are not open to the public per se but if you are interested in joining, contact library staff, who will provide you with additional information.

The librarian may want to ask the book group leader, or the member with whom the librarian has been dealing vis-à-vis the book club's use of library facilities, if he or she would appreciate the librarian attending the first meeting that is held under the library's roof to speak to the group. Explaining library policies concerning the book group's "behavior" is only a small portion of what the librarian's talk would consist of; the primary purpose would be to establish good public relations in the form of showing to the group what services the library can provide the members, such as available reference sources useful to locating further information on an author and helpful in locating reviews of the particular book that will be discussed at the upcoming meeting. Of course, this falls under the heading of "outreach services" and will contribute to a healthy rapport between the library and the community.

The other services that a librarian may choose to extend to a book club that has arranged to meet in your library would be securing copies of the discussion books for all the members. Chances are, no matter what book, nonfiction or fiction, the group may have chosen, there will be not be enough copies in the library's collection to cover the entire group. In fact, there may be only a single copy. Given the state of bookstores these days—by which I mean the *scarcity* of bookstores these days—most group members will order their copy from Amazon. But wouldn't it make a great public relations gesture to volunteer to order copies for everyone, for every book in the club's schedule for discussion, through your jobber? And give them the library discount. Details would need to be worked out with your jobber, but this gesture is definitely something to talk about.

A "Homegrown" Book Club

Ordering copies of the book under discussion for every member is a good idea for extending a welcome to an "outside" book group that meets within your library's four walls. But it's an even better idea—an actual enticement, that is—when you the organizing librarian are organizing your *own* book group from scratch. That means the librarian is not simply supplying space to a book group that pretty much functions on its own, but rather you the librarian are sponsoring that group in the library in order to lead it. If you let readers know that anyone who signs up for your book group will get discounted copies of the books, then interest will probably be high. Of course, what you would have to protect against are the people who have no intention of participating in the group discussion but simply want a copy of the book for a price cheaper than they would otherwise be able to obtain it. More about that later.

Now, the direction that our book club discussion must take is a natural and necessary exploration of all the benefits and issues involved in "growing" one's own book club in a library setting. The grower—the developer, if you prefer a less metaphoric label—is the public librarian. The librarian's involvement is, of course, at a higher level than what is experienced when extending your library's space for a book group that for the most part will be left to its own devices, but doing so under the comforting and even inspiring roof of your library.

Starting a book group from the ground up entails considerably more—and more intense—factors to not only reflect on but also, after decisions about them have been made, to then act on them. For a librarian to develop a book discussion group in his or her library is to move up the ladder of book and author programming in energy and time and expertise expenditure and in personal and professional responsibility. Like a law of nature, however, the more involved a book or author program is, the higher the level of dividends, both professional and personal, awarded to the librarian and the library itself.

One Approach

The guidance we will be proffering, with suggestions for the organization and operation of a book group and warnings of situations to avoid, and above all the tone of encouragement we hope our whole discussion is wrapped in as we lead the librarian through the processes and procedures of forming a book club and successfully executing its purpose (which is, of course, getting good books read and discussed), will begin by underscoring the necessity of efficiency, with the librarian posing a set of important procedural questions to which she or he needs to arrive at answers for, to ensure a good experience suitable for everyone's needs and expectations.

We will first address some important procedural questions vital to forming a book group in your library. The first question is one we previously addressed when discussing a library that is just hosting a group: Where do the copies of the books under discussion come from? As a good public relations measure, I suggested the librarian order copies for everyone from their jobber and extend the discount to club members. But I would also encourage readers to borrow from other libraries they may have a connection with and access to (with the caveat that copies borrowed from libraries cannot be written in; so if the club member likes to notetake while reading, a pad at hand will be necessary); and encourage group members to comb local used bookstores, where copies can be found often at remarkable discount, and obviously, since they are now in your possession, can be written in, underlined, and all the other ways you personalize and enhance your reading experiences.

Discussion Leader

Who is to be the discussion leader? The obvious answer that springs to mind is *you*. As the local librarian, you have formed the group, or at least you are in the process of getting one formed, have the right and perhaps the obligation to lead—at least until the group is off the ground and you've gotten familiar with group members and know which ones can be counted on to maintain good attendance and, at the same time, have demonstrated the ability to discuss books in a proficient manner. But, for the time being, while you the organizing librarian are in the *process* of organizing your group, the best way to plan is to answer that you will be the discussion leader for quite some time. and then build your group and its practices accordingly. At a later point—in just a few pages—we will address the all-important issue of how to select a good book club book, but right now there are more pressing, more fundamental factors to decide on.

What Size Book Group?

Right away, you need to decide how large or small a group you want. I recommend ten to twenty members be allowed in, and then the club be closed off to more new members, with a waiting list being maintained. The issue with size is this: too large a group and discussion gets too loose and baggy, with individuals maybe getting in one or two comments, or the discussion falling to two or three people who are the most domineering. (Of course, if you decide that your book group is going to be open to any and all of your library patrons or members of the community who have chosen to read the book and show up at the designated time, and open the floor to anyone who wants to speak—good luck with that! The difficulty with this type of "club" is that keeping the discussion on track is difficult. You are bound to have people go off on thoughts about their personal experiences that are only thinly germane to the book at hand, or worse, someone who has shown up not intending to discuss the book but rather to rail against it or the author, often without having actually read the book!)

On the other hand, with too small a group, the discussion may peter out quickly, without a sufficient number of contributions to keep things flowing. People may feel too intimidated to speak when there are only, say, two other people. They may feel it a burden to have lots to say and to say it articulately. (But too large a group, too, can easily intimidate members, because performance anxiety syndrome is at play before a big audience.) Another factor to keep in mind when deciding on an appropriate size is to have enough "padding"—i.e., enough members to still have a good discussion size when absences occur—and they will!

Who Chooses the Books?

Will the group be entirely *yours*—meaning, is the choosing of books to be read and discussed to be left up to you, to be your prerogative? Initially, yes. Again, until the group gets going and settles into a cohesive whole, "order" is best maintained when you the librarian as group leader select the books. Until you know the group members better and the other members get better acquainted, too much time will be spent proposing and disagreeing and re-suggesting, without the real purpose—discussing good books among good readers who have interesting points to make—being gotten to in a timely fashion. No, for the time being at least, and perhaps indefinitely, *you* select the books to be read and discussed. How to select good ones? We will address that in a minute.

What Kind of Books?

Of course, the question of who is selecting the books naturally leads to an important issue needing addressing right away; it requires a decision to be made quickly after the idea of starting a book club in your library. That issue is, What kind of book club? Will your book group be ecumenical in types and topics? Or will you and your readers lean strictly toward fiction or toward nonfiction or will you maintain a balance of the two? How about gearing you and your readers toward a certain genre of fiction? After all, crime fiction is perennially popular, and I met—well, I encountered her as a participant in a recent *Booklist* webinar on book clubs—a public librarian who keeps two mystery book clubs going in her library, like having two plates spinning simultaneously. Obviously, if you are starting a niche reading group and are not especially well-versed in the genre or subject matter, you'll need to consult someone on your library staff who has good background information, or at least you'll need to use online reference sources to gain fundamental information, including, if it's fiction and you are having the group read and discuss, who are the important authors.

Women's fiction might be an agreeable choice for a large group of readers, but it hardly seems worth mentioning—but I will do so—that, if that is the focus your group will take, you should be prepared to *not* entice male club members.

The kind of books you can choose, in defining your group, comprises a large list, indeed, but I advise you not to be too narrow and restrictive. Yes, a niche situation will attract readers devoted to that subject or genre, and will attract them with gusto, but at the same time you won't be extending a very wide appeal to a great range of readers. (I would hazard a guess that mystery book clubs are the safest niche to organize and be guaranteed a good turnout.)

How to Select a Book

You've determined what kind of books your group "will be about." Now comes a more challenging aspect of the situation, which is also a very interesting part of organizing and maintaining a book group: What criteria go into selecting the actual titles to read? Essentially, then, we need to now establish some guiding principles for determining what makes a successful book club book.

First of all, I posit that a book group does *not* have to discuss only very recent books. Older titles, even *old* titles (if they are still in print, of course), should be given their due, for they can bring enlightenment and excitement to the reader even if the books are long past being hot off the press. Classic titles would not be defined as such if they had not stood the test of time and had admirers generation after generation; and nonfiction topics, if topical, have a shorter shelf life than fiction, but even nonfiction—I'm thinking of memoir, specifically, at this moment—has relevance for you after publication. Again, the key is your flexibility. In other words, don't box yourself in with a bunch of unnecessary rules. But, on the other hand, don't tackle anything incredibly outdated unless that is the point of reading and discussing it in the first place: to put a historical perspective on the subject, that is. For instance, when it comes to science, be careful of much older titles, unless, again, they are classics as "literature," such as Charles Darwin's *The Origin of Species*. You read that book now not for its exact science but for its historical importance.

The idea may occur to you as the organizer and session leader to start "small" and work up in "size." By "small" I mean a short book that, if fiction, presents a limited, unelaborate plot and only a few rather easy-to-comprehend characters;

and if nonfiction, covers a limited segment of the world's knowledge on a given subject. To that sentiment I issue an emphatic *no!* You're not teaching someone how to walk. No baby steps are required or even advised. Jump in at the deep end of the pool, as it were. The point of a book discussion group is to encourage and cultivate a *discussion*.

How Do You Know If It's a Book-Club Kind of Book?

First of all, you have to weigh limited appeal against wide appeal. The books you choose should fall somewhere in between, on a spectrum that ranges from '0'— which are books most people would consider fluff—to '10,' which are books that, if nonfiction, are academic titles for professional reading and, if fiction, are highly experimental or have the reputation of being time-consuming and difficult to follow, to the degree of appealing only to a small group of literature lovers.

Fine-tuning where your group's interest falls in the easy vs. difficult spectrum will happen as time goes by; it may come to pass, in an almost evolutionary fashion, that the group will trend toward harder or easier books, without announcing any official decision in that regard.

If the book was occasional, in that it is nonfiction and written about some recent natural disaster or political crisis or medical crisis (for instance, the Zika virus scare as I write this), the interest level for that book is bound to be high (let's face it, readers who join a book group are usually followers of the news and appreciate in-depth coverage of such events). So get those titles on your list right away, and place them early in your line-up schedule. Now, peruse the book and read early reviews to make certain the book is a responsible treatment of the subject. Journalism is fine, just be sure it's *fine* journalism.

Again, if you are selecting nonfiction, choose a book with a definite point of view: the stronger the tack taken by the author the more conversation within a book group will be aroused. Encourage politeness and regard for differing opinions, but at the same time encourage legitimate disagreement—disagreement not stemming from insult. And, again, I place on your shoulders the responsibility for knowing if the book you are thinking of adding to your group's discussion list qualifies as "diatribe," defined by Merriam-Webster as an "angry and usually long speech or piece of history that strongly criticizes someone or something." Should you avoid a book—usually in this context, a nonfiction book—that you realize, either by getting involved in its pages or by sampling advance notices, is indeed a diatribe? I'm not saying that at all. What I am saying is that know it as a diatribe and recognize what kind of offense the book may cause in your group.

Mein Kampf

An article in the *New York Times* Op-Ed page for July 8, 2014 (*The New York Times*, July 8, 2014, "Should Germans Read 'Mein Kampf'?" by Peter Ross Range) revealed that after many years of suppressing the publication of Adolf Hitler's memoir/diatribe, the government of the German state of Bavaria, which has held the copyright and has up to this point refused the book's republication, will soon lose the copyright. And that will mean anyone will soon be able to publish the book. The point of the *New York Times* editorial was that this is a good thing. The book is available in other countries—purchased easily—so why should Germans not be able to read it and in that big way confront the full aspect of their historical past?

Would I place *Mein Kampf* on a list of titles I would suggest as a suitable conversation starter in a book-club situation? I would not. On the other hand, I do not believe in censorship in any form, and if a librarian has a very sophisticated reading-group interest in twentieth-century history and learning all about Communism and Nazism, then practice what I've preached: Understand completely what you're doing if you should select *Mein Kampf* for group discussion.

Book-Club Worthy?

Let me interject an idea I feel is of primary importance in book selection for a reading group. And that is to ask yourself, "Is this book book-club worthy?" In other words, will the club members take away from the book an experience that deepens to some extent their reactions to the world, and will it prompt a discussion that members will see as not a waste of time? If *Mein Kampf* is club-worthy in your estimation, then proceed. But when this question will come into play more often and more relevantly is toward the other end of the difficulty/appeal spectrum I previously talked about. Is this celebrity memoir too breezy to be club-worthy? Is this novel really too popular—popular as in pot-boilerish—to connect to serious readers and give them a sense of having learned a little bit more about the human condition?

If the book you are considering as a candidate is nonfiction, is it worth the time taken to read it for what you learn about the topic? A longish book not complicated to read nevertheless, because of the number of its pages, still requires longish reading time. The question is, then, is the topic covered in a degree correlative to the book's great length? If it's a slim book—around a hundred pages or even less—then the question is, is it still worth the time—not nearly as much time, obviously—or is the coverage so superficial that readers come away virtually empty-handed and thus, in book-club terms, will there be enough to talk about?

If the book you want to consider for book-club discussion is fiction, you'll need to consider if the novel lies strictly on an entertainment level, or does it also have artistic merit. I think it would not surprise you at this point in reading the book you have in your hands that I advocate fiction that can keep reader's constant attention but at the same time holds within its arsenal of good qualities an abundance of artistry. A novel that stands with legs on both these levels is book-club worthy, capable of generating a good discussion that has many possibilities for directions to take. Usually leaning toward fiction that is high on the literary scale means you and your members will have a richer vein to mine.

Short Fiction

I am a great lover of the short story and a rabid advocate of that form's reading pleasure and the need for more widespread appreciation of what short stories have to offer. After all, my favorite contemporary fiction writer is Alice Munro, whose Nobel-honored career is based on her work in the short story, and my all-time favorite fiction writer is Eudora Welty, who, of course, while the author of several high-grade novels, including the Pulitzer Prize–winning *The Optimist's Daughter*, achieved her renown primality through her highly distinctive short stories.

So, I take this opportunity to stand on my soapbox and issue a plea to any and all librarians who are forming book clubs and selecting the books to be read and discussed to include on their reading list a collection of short stories. A bitter pill for club members to swallow? I certainly don't believe so. The whole point of a book discussion group is to broaden and strengthen member's' reading experiences. Bring in the short story to achieve such a broadening. I suggest selecting a short story writer who is big and popular today and has a reputation as a short-fiction writer who draws in readers who are not sure they are necessarily lovers of the form. And who better than Alice Munro?

Background to Nonfiction

Speaking again of nonfiction, a question to ask yourself about a possible book for group discussion is whether the book takes the reader well into the subject, which it should do to be book-club material; but at the same time does the book require more than commonly held background knowledge on the subject? Even the advisability of doing some online research beforehand may be too much "homework" for the typical book-club member. Keep that in mind. If your group members are eager learners of new information, then no problem will stand in the way of most of them needing to "background" themselves before starting the book, or at least before the discussion itself.

Hand in hand with this idea of extra "work" is the question of whether a nonfiction book you are considering adds something more or new to the body of information. Are there just too many books out there on the subject or does this one fill an information gap? Or at least does it present the information in a new way, with a new approach, and with a new conclusion worth considering; or at least does it present a relatively complex topic in terms not diluted but accessible and comprehensible to the general reader?

Broad Approach to Fiction

When deciding on what novels to add to your discussion list, think about this: Don't crowd—clog—your list with famous names and books, either past or contemporary, to the exclusion of more obscure—but still very good, of course—writers who deserve their due by being read closely and discussed closely in book clubs. This, naturally, calls for careful screening. You don't want a book to be obscure for a reason (meaning, deserving its obscurity because the work just isn't that good). Obscurity is defined by deserving wider attention than it's received, for reasons unknown, other than too many good books are out there vying for the public's attention and some outstanding ones just get overlooked. This is a great role for book clubs to step into: bringing a handful of those books to your group's attention.

Joyce Saricks is currently the audio editor at *Booklist*. Previously, she ran the Readers' Advisory department at the Downers Grove (IL) Public Library, and she has served as an adjunct professor in the Graduate School of Library and Information Science at Dominican University. She is the author of two ALA Editions books, *The Readers' Advisory Guide to Genre Fiction* (2009) and *Readers' Advisory Service in the Public Library* (2005).

Book clubs in the library? Are sponsoring them or organizing them worth the librarian's efforts for good library promotion?

I've always argued that book discussions are the most expensive programs libraries offer. The staff time is tremendous: time to read (and to read with an eye toward discovering discussion points, not simply for pleasure), to formulate questions, to collect background material on the author and book, and finally to run the discussion. I blame Oprah. Once she started her book club, it was almost impossible for a library not to have one, too, either to run one themselves, to offer space for discussions, or to create kits with copies of books and questions for checkout.

What problems in organizing and presenting book clubs have you encountered?

Finding a format that works can be problematic. When I first started [library work] in the mid-1970s, I offered four titles at each discussion. Subsequently, we read only one book (sometimes paired with a movie). The problem that concerned me most was how to attract men to the group. Even when we read fiction by men, we had little success, except for an occasional husband. My library now offers a nonfiction book discussion as well, and that attracts men and many couples. I never discovered the secret formula to attract men to our fiction discussions.

Based on your experience, what advice would you give facilitator librarians for a smooth-running book club?

Know your group and choose titles they will enjoy—or at least enjoy discussing. Encourage them to offer suggestions for titles to discuss, but if you are leading the discussion you should make the final decision. Some titles simply aren't discussible. Bring more questions than you think you'll need—or be prepared with material related to the discussion. Nonfiction materials to complement historically set novels, for example. Or DVDs of interest to the topic. Or bring a stack of books to book talk and share. There are few situations more fraught than finishing your questions 30 minutes into a 90-minute discussion. In addition to questions that are related to your book, keep a list of generic questions: What does the title mean? Are there loose ends that are unresolved?

The first consideration is to find out if the novel you are interested in, one that falls into the category of underserved obscurity, remains in print. If not, it is probably not a suitable choice for your reading list. But before that—let's back up here—you need to learn what some of these books are. You have your memory and your readers' advisory skills and notebooks and files to help you. You have the past five years, say, of year-old "best of" lists from, among other sources, and *good* sources, the library review media, including *Booklist*'s Editors' Choice lists, appearing in every January issue and covering the previous year.

As you run your eyes down these lists and scan the annotations accompanying each title, you will recognize the titles that were "big" and those that, despite being applauded as good quality by editorial staffs, never made it big in terms of best-seller lists and word-of-mouth, or even literary prizes. But you can bet they remain as top-notch reads as any number of their best-lists-mates.

Prize Lists

I recently served as chair of the Carnegie selection committee, an American Library Association–sponsored award given every year to an outstanding work of fiction and work of nonfiction (along with two finalists in each category). The medal (the awards are in the form of a Medal of Excellence) are now in their sixth year, and I boast that the winners of the past five years and the finalists that comprised the awards list are outstanding books *and* outstanding for book groups. The Carnegie Committee is comprised of librarians active in the American Library Association and editors at *Booklist* magazine, from ALA, and consequently the medal winners reflect not only the Committee members' critical acumen but also their second-nature ability to consider the relevance of every nominated book to the well-read public library patron. Consulting the list of previous winners and "runners-up," the organizer of a book club in the library couldn't ask for better suggestions for inclusion on their list of good candidates for book club reading and discussion.

A coworker of mine belongs to an extremely high-end book club: meaning, their choices for reading and discussion are consistently high-end in terms of content and treatment. They've made it a procedural point to every year read a book by that year's Nobel Prize winner in literature. That, of course, has given them quite a range of reading material, from fiction to poetry to drama; but these authors and their often strange works have provided interesting discussions.

So, what these comments are leading to is my suggestion that to begin a discussion group, you might lean heavily at first on the prize winners, which include, along with the above-mentioned Carnegie Medals and Nobel Prize in Literature, the Pulitzer Prize, the National Book Award, and the National Book Critics' Circle winner. It goes nearly without saying, but I insist on saying it nevertheless, that the group selections should not stick to the prize list by any means. Use them as a place to start and a place to augment your list as time goes on with books that distinguished readers have found to be first-rate in quality.

Ultimate Consideration: Storytelling

Above and beyond all, there is the most outstanding, most crucial, most definite quality of a book-club worthy book: *robust storytelling*. Whether fiction or nonfiction, the book must exhibit in bold and unhesitant terms a narrative drive that will compel the widest spectrum of readers through its pages from start to finish. A book-club worthy book, whether a novel or a book that is factual, is a book written by an author who shows through his life-filled prose and, importantly, his attitude toward what stirs the hearts of readers to cry out, "Yes, this is truth. This is goodness. This is a book to get inside of and dwell in for many days. This book will be my temporary home."

NOTES

1. Nathan Heller, "Book Clubs: Why Do We Love Them So Much?" Slate.com, July 29, 2011.
2. Barbara Brotman, "Queen of Clubs." *Chicago Tribune*, Lifetime section, May 30, 2001.

Chapter Three

Book Clubs, Part II

BOOK DISCUSSION BEST PRACTICES

So, you've put your shoulder to the grindstone and, based on sound and creative selection principles, have come up with a list of books you are certain would be good conversation-inducers for your book group. You are certain you can propose these titles to the members and get a good reception.

Now, we need to address another significant step in the development of your group: how to discuss a book. I can't emphasize enough the importance of you, as group leader, performing well in this regard. The success of your book group depends on it. As we will see, the discussion leader needs to probe well beyond the clichéd, "Did you like the book?"

To begin with, the leader needs to suggest at the outset of your meetings, at an introductory meeting if you have scheduled one, that members come to every session armed with approximately a dozen questions—by which I mean, of course, discussion points. After all, you the discussion leader need to be able to come to each session comfortable that the allotted discussion time will be filled with meaningful conversation. In addition, the group members need to have an abiding sense of your subtle but effective ability to direct the group in a direction that will enable the members to get the most out of a reading experience.

Act Like a Sheepdog

Consequently, like an intelligent, well-bred sheepherding dog, you will need to be vigilant in steering the group in the desired direction, and by "the desired direction," I mean, of course, maintain relevance to the book and its contents. More specifically and practically, I'm taking aim at tangents: they must be firmly guided away from. Another canine metaphor: Don't let someone in the group grab the conversational ball in their mouth and take off across the field. The bad result of that is that people might forget where the real discussion was before the rude interruption and the good flow is lost. I'm all for interrupting someone who has embarked on a tangent with, "Show us how that relates to the book or the author." Say it in a way that is not confrontational but in a tone generally indicating legitimate interest. Even better is if you the discussion leader perceive the existence of a kernel of "useful" (relevant) information somewhere within the tangent—that is, a legitimately appropriate opinion expressed by the speaker as part of his or her tangent—and say, "Let's go back to something you said. Please elaborate on——." And it is hoped the discussion gets back on track in the desired direction.

Let me say unequivocally that tangents, which tend to be personal expositions, are essentially "all about me" and simply cannot be tolerated. Time is short and precious, especially if you have a sizable membership, and tangents are time-consuming. There is even a risk of losing club members.

About the Author

I would suggest that at the outset of every discussion session the leader begin things by giving some background information on the author. Nothing greatly detailed but sufficient for all members to appreciate the author's previous works, positions held, and awards received. This information can be turned into an effective discussion starter. For instance, knowing where the author grew up, what in this book reflects that environment? Now knowing the author's previous novels, how do you see this book fitting into her oeuvre? The author is a newspaper reporter, so do you see his line of work informing the type of material he writes about and the style he uses? Are you surprised this author just won the Nobel Prize, and if so, why?

The possibilities of author-related questions establishing a good basis for discussion range widely.

It's Just an Opinion

When I gave book-review-writing workshops to librarians or when I used to break in a new freelance reviewer for *Booklist*, one of the points I stressed is that reviewing is just expressing an opinion—*your* opinion, of course, and that has its worth— but not *gospel* truth. There is *no* gospel truth in reviewing, be it reviewing books, movies, or plays. To give an opinion on a book is only that: an *opinion*. Now, hopefully your opinion is based on knowledge and perception. In other words, stemming from an experienced perspective: experienced in reading and critiquing.

How does that translate into our discussion about book clubs? When it boils down to it, offering comments about a book in a discussion group is not different than writing a review. You are entitled to your opinion; *everyone* is entitled to an opinion. Opinions can be challenged, which, of course, is the meat of a book discussion group. But opinions expressed by other people should never be dismissed, even opinions that one may find too extreme or too far-fetched or too weak. That is where book groups differ from the pages of a magazine or newspaper, print version or online. You can disagree with what you read and mentally deride the reviewer's opinion, and you can even write a letter to the editor (print sources always have a website with an e-mail facility) and express your disagreement or even outrage. Writers of reviews must take it in stride—it comes with the territory—that they will face unacceptance of their critical opinion. (It occurs to me that people who "write in" do so generally to cross swords rather than to compliment and support.)

But book discussion groups? There is a different protocol at play here. Or there *should* be a different protocol. As you can see, my attitude is that the tenor of a book club should be based on the outwardly simple dictum of disagree, yes, but dismiss, no. It may sound too smaltzy to some, but I insist that in a relatively small group of people, feelings count. Hurt feelings—the kind that can easily result from dismissed opinions—can impede discussion and sink the sessions into awkwardness. People don't join a book club to be belittled; being challenged, on the other hand, can sharpen your opinions or open your mind to possible alternative ways of thinking.

And, of course, out-and-out arguing is way out of the question. Must I even say that? There is simply no point or productiveness to an argument.

On the other hand, facts recognized as inaccurate that are placed before the group *should* be called out as such, regardless if these "facts" introduced are pertinent to the topics in a nonfiction book or to characters or plot in a novel. But an appropriate "correction" voice should be used, such as "I think you mean. . . ." When an opinion to which you cannot subscribe is presented, you are welcome to present your contradictory opinion, but always in a calm, civil voice.

It's inevitable that some of your group participants will see competition in every aspect of book discussion—just as they see competition pretty much everywhere, especially because a book discussion situation will feel like an intellectual competition to the competitive type of personality. Regardless, this "mentality" should be discouraged, at least within the context of the discussion group you've founded and are leading. Say it at the first session and repeat it in later sessions as necessary: your estimation of a book, while valuable to the group, is only an opinion, not the gospel truth. Listen to other people's ideas. Their opinions are important to the group, too. This is the very dynamic that holds a book discussion group together.

Two Vitally Important Questions

At this point in our discussion of how to discuss a book, I'd like to bring up a concept that I propose will make a big difference in organizing your thoughts about a book—specifically, in preparation for a group discussion. When I am instructing a group of librarians about how to write reviews, I offer that every review, long or short, must answer two questions: (1) What is the book about? and (2) How good is it? Every review is based on these two points. Find a review close at hand, in a newspaper or a library magazine. Read it. Aren't I correct? No matter where the review takes you, everything stated—everything in a well-expressed review, that is—is in answer to what the book is about and how good it is. It's inevitable, it's as close to a formula as a well-done review comes close to being. But a workable, even necessary, formula. A formula that doesn't render every review too close in content and approach to every other review.

That pertains to book clubs as well, in the following fashion: the double-question that every review has to answer—what is the book about, how good is it—is an almost ideal way to structure your thoughts about a book that you are reading for a book group. Let your note-taking fall into those two categories. You'll find that in leading a discussion you will want to discuss both questions, whether you have a novel or a nonfiction book in hand. And I would be so bold as to suggest to you that *you* suggest to your group members to ask themselves those two questions for every book read by the group, and to encourage your members to organize their notes—or at least their thoughts—thusly; consequently, they will come to discussion night with a firm approach to knowing how to begin discussing the book being focused on that particular evening.

But, of course, that leads to the next issue: members need to know *how* to answer the two questions.

But First . . .

Let me reiterate a piece of advice I've already proffered. It is not mandatory—but close to being so—but I highly recommend that the discussion leader lead off every discussion with a profile of the book's author. Brief research can provide you with such. What you *don't* want to do is simply read aloud the author bio that comes with the book, especially that which is found on the cover of the paperback edition. No, do your own composing. Hit such specific topics as what kind of works the author is known for and awards that the author has been given, but don't go on too long. Two, three minutes will be fine. You are really just cracking the ice so that the discussion can begin.

But keep in mind that the author's bio you shared with the group may prompt a first discussion point. Depending on the author and the book he or she has written, you may supply yourself with an opening discussion question with something like: "He's from rural Georgia. What about that environment obviously informs what his book is about?" But, of course, I plead for variety. Yes, begin each discussion with an author introduction, but don't in every instance launch the discussion with an author-related question. You don't want every book discussion session to be like every other session.

Back To . . .

We've established the advisability of answering the two important questions when thinking and talking about a book. But, now, let's examine just how to go *about* answering those two questions; how to arrive at practical and specific ways of providing answers, and consequently allow you to proceed through a book discussion with flying colors. Now, I must make it clear—again—that a discussion certainly does not have to follow any certain pattern or template. What I mean is that as a discussion leader you need not start with the exact question, "What is the book about?" and exhaust all aspects of that topic, then move on to "How good is it?" and analyze every angle of that question. Discussions soon take on a life of their own, and as long as the discussion ultimately and in its own fashion answers the two questions, give the discussion free rein and allow it to develop its own "personality." (But remember my warning against tangents!)

Shame on you if you maintain a rigid book discussion group. But praise to you if you run a well-organized one.

Back To . . . Again. . . .

Let's return to my point in the previous paragraph. Just how do you go about concretely answering the two "big" questions and thus arrive at meaty, worthy discussion questions and points?

Let's present a "case" of nonfiction first. "What is the book about?" can be briefly or fully answered as desired or need be, but the real point is that an answer should not be difficult to come by. If it is, the book is perhaps too esoteric for a general book group. Take Doris Kearns Goodwin's recent *Bully Pulpit*. What is it about? Briefly, it's about Presidents Teddy Roosevelt and William Howard Taft and the Progressive Era in American politics. To me, the next question to ask once the subject of a nonfiction book has been established, with all members satisfied with what has been put on the table in terms of defining the book's subject, is then to pose the question, "And what is the author's point of view on that subject?" In the case of Goodwin's *Bully Pulpit*, we have a three-part authorial perspective: her view of Roosevelt, of Taft, and of the muckraking press so active in that era.

If your designated book for this discussion session is a novel, I would suggest this as an initial conversation starter: "Who wants to give us a brief synopsis of what happens in the book?" The follow up, as I see it, would be, "That's the basic plot. What is the novel's basic theme? And how does theme differ from plot?" OK, let's back up. Truth be told, theme is not an easily determined defining characteristic of a novel for readers unused to fiction criticism. You as group leader may have to define "theme" before the group can have a productive conversation about

Other Books and Authors

Finally, to draw the discussion to a productive close, the leader can address the ever-popular topic of similar books and authors. This is where group members like to shine—to polish up their image as someone very well read; and this is where a high degree of helpfulness is brought into the group discussion, because everyone gets something out of other good readers making book-and-author connections. As discussion leader, make certain that the connections are explained, more than just simply, "You'll like this one, too."

I would say that connections should be tight and specific—meaning, for a novel, a plot connection should be based on a great similarity in plot; character connections based on, say, the *same* historical personage. The author's style—I'm not certain that is always a strong connection. In terms of making connections between nonfiction books, the primary one, of course, is subject matter. If the group is discussing a Civil War book, the connection could be to a good biography of Confederate president Jefferson Davis (for instance, *Jefferson Davis, American* by William J. Cooper). I would suggest to your group that their proffered connections between nonfiction books also be made by subject matter; any other connections lead too far afield and may not be meaningful to the group.

All kidding aside, other connections, for both fiction and nonfiction, should not rest simply on, "If you liked this guy, you'll like that guy." Be specific: What about this author closely resembles the other author. For nonfiction, it isn't good enough to say, "She reminds me of this other author." In what specific ways? And if the specific ways are not solid enough, your group members will let that recommendation go in one ear and out the other.

In other words, to bring up a connection to the book being discussed and make it stick—by which I mean, lodge in group member's memories or worth jotting down into a pocket notebook—it needs to be a strong, creative one, or why bother?

Award-Winning Book Discussion Guides

The Notable Books Council of the American Library Association's Reference and Users Services Association, charged with compiling an annual list of notable books for use of the general adult reader, devised a set of book-group discussion questions for the 2014 winners of the Andrew Carnegie Medals for Excellence in Fiction and Nonfiction, Doris Kearns Goodwin's *The Bully Pulpit* for the latter and Donna Tartt's *The Goldfinch* for the former.

But, first, let me share the *Booklist* reviews of these two Andrew Carnegie Medal-winning books, to acquaint readers who may have no previous familiarity.

The Bully Pulpit: Theodore Roosevelt, William Howard Taft, and the Golden Age of Journalism, by Doris Kearns Goodwin. Simon & Schuster.

"In this hyperpartisan era, it is well to remember that a belief in an activist federal government that promoted both social and economic progress crossed party lines, as it did during the Progressive movement of the early twentieth century. Goodwin, the acclaimed historian, repeatedly emphasizes that fact in her massive and masterful study of the friendship, and then enmity, of two presidents who played major roles in that movement. Roosevelt, unsurprisingly, is portrayed by Goodwin as egotistical, bombastic, and determined to take on powerful special interests. He saw his secretary of war, Taft, as a friend and disciple. Then Taft, as president, seemed to abandon the path of reform, Roosevelt saw it as both a political and a personal betrayal. Taft, sadly remembered by many as our fattest president, receives nuanced, sympathetic, but not particularly favorable treatment here. But this is also an examination of some of the great journalists who exposed societal ills and promoted the reformers that aimed to address them. Many of these "muckrakers," including Ida Tarbell and Lincoln Steffens, worked for *McClure's* Magazine. This is a superb recreation of a period when many politicians, journalists, and citizens of differing political affiliations viewed government as a force for public good." (Jay Freeman)

Discussion questions for *The Bully Pulpit: Theodore Roosevelt, William Howard Taft, and the Golden Age of Journalism:*

1. Name several comparisons between the Progressive Era and today. Would you rather be a member of the working class then or now? Who is a contemporary robber baron in your opinion?
2. What was the role of the press then? What is it now? How do they compare? Who is doing the muckraking (reform-minded journalism) of today?
3. Talk about the women in this book. What roles did they take on and play at home and in politics?
4. How has your view of Theodore Roosevelt changed since reading this book? Could a modern president do what he did while in office?

5. This is a story of friendship and rivalry. Which other U.S. presidents have experienced both friendship and rivalry?

6. Goodwin could not have written such an intimate portrait of the two men without their letters to each other and to their wives. How will history be recorded for historians in the next 100 years?

7. Goodwin has noted that Ida Tarbell knew how to make people come to life on the page. How does Goodwin manage to do the same?

8. Steven Spielberg and DreamWorks, the makers of the movie *Lincoln*, based in part on Goodwin's *Team of Rivals*, have acquired the rights to make a film based on *The Bully Pulpit*. How different would this movie be from *Lincoln*? Whom would you cast for the parts of Teddy Roosevelt, William Taft, Alice Lee Roosevelt, Edith Roosevelt, Nellie Taft, Ida Tarbell, and Sam McClure? What scenes from *The Bully Pulpit* stick out in your mind as particularly cinematic?

9. The role of government in dealing with the economic and social issues was as central an issue during the Progressive Era as it is today. What do you think Roosevelt would say about the social and economic issues of today?

10. The text of this book is 750 pages. Did the detail incorporated into this volume advance or detract from the story? If you could edit, what would you cut? Is there an untold story here, something you would have liked more of?

11. Goodwin has confessed that the Progressive Era was her favorite time in history. If she were to write another biography, whom would you like it to be about?

The Goldfinch, by Donna Tartt. Little, Brown

"Cataclysmic loss and rapture with criminal intent visited upon the young have been Tartt's epic subjects as she creates one captivating and capacious novel a decade, from *The Secret History* (1992) to *The Little Friend* (2002) to this feverish saga. In the wake of his nefarious father's abandonment, Theo, a smart, 13-year-old Manhattanite, is extremely close to his vivacious mother—until an act of terrorism catapults him into a dizzying world bereft of gravity, certainty, and love. Tartt writes from Theo's point of view with fierce exactitude and magnetic emotion as, stricken with grief and post-traumatic stress syndrome, he seeks sanctuary with a troubled Park Avenue family and, in Greenwich Village, with a kind and gifted restorer of antique furniture. Fate then delivers Theo to utterly alien Las Vegas, where he meets young outlaw Boris. As Theo becomes a completely damaged adult, Tartt, in a boa constrictor-like plot, pulls him deeply into the shadow lands of art, lashed to seventeenth-century Dutch artist Carel Fabritius and his exquisite if sinister painting, *The Goldfinch*. Drenched in sensory detail, infused with Theo's churning thoughts and feelings, sparked by nimble dialogue, and propelled by escalating cosmic angst and thriller action, Tartt's trenchant, defiant, engrossing, and rocketing novel conducts a grand inquiry into the mystery and sorrow of survival, beauty and obsession, and the promise of art." (Donna Seaman)

Discussion questions for *The Goldfinch* by Donna Tartt:

1. Tartt has noted that the purposeful destruction of the giant sandstone Buddhas of Bamiyan Valley Afghanistan in March 2001 inspired her to begin her novel with an explosion. Does this statement, by Theo's mother, speak to this?: "People die, sure," my mother was saying, "But it's so heartbreaking and unnecessary how we lose things. From pure carelessness. Fires, wars. The Parthenon, used as a munitions storehouse. I guess that anything we manage to save from history is a miracle." Talk about the lost, recovery, and loss and recovery again of the painting *The Goldfinch*. Is it a miracle? What else is lost in this story?

2. How many ways is Theo tied to the Goldfinch, which is "forced, always, to land in the same hopeless place." What are the similarities between the aching of the boy and the chains on the bird?

3. Coincidentally, Fabritius's painting *The Goldfinch* came to New York City and opened at the Frick on the same day Tartt's book was released. Also coincidentally, Tartt received the Andrew Carnegie Medal for Excellence in Fiction in Las Vegas in June 2014. Some readers have expressed public dismay about the rather long middle section of the book that takes place in Las Vegas. Do you think this section was important? Why or why not?

4. For an orphan, Theo actually participated in a number of flawed family units. What were the advantages and disadvantages of each?

5. In the tradition of the Bildungsroman, we observe Theo's growth and development. Pippa is sure he is suffering from PTSD. What evidence do we have that Theo actually grows out of his 13-year-old self?

6. Theo asks how can you follow your heart if your heart cannot be trusted. Are there situations in this story where you would advise him to follow his heart? His head? Why?

7. Stephen King called *The Goldfinch* a smartly written literary novel. In the sense that great art is timeless, what clues do you get about the time period in which the story takes place, and do these references (Bon Jovi, iPods) make it more or less likely that the book itself will become a classic in a future literary canon?

8. There are many literary references in this book, not the least of which is Boris' habit of calling Theo "Potter." What are some similarities between Theo and Harry? Or Theo and Oliver Twist? Or Pippa and Estella from Dickens' *Great Expectations*? Can you find more similarities with literary themes? For example, the theme of unrequited love?

9. If you read for language, you will have found some beautiful passages in this book. Reviewers have called it "flawless," "sparkling," "eloquent and assured." Do you have a favorite paragraph, or one to share? How do you feel about the attention to detail her descriptions of people, places, and situations offer?

10. What connections do you read into the fact that Hobie calls his remade furniture "changelings"? Tartt uses that phrase in relation to Xerox machines and "the line of beauty." Talk about art and imitation.

11. Read these two sentences and discuss where this "place" is, which she calls the "rainbow edge" and "polychrome edge":

> "Between reality on the one hand, and the point where the mind strikes reality, there's a middle zone, a rainbow edge, where beauty comes into being, where two different surfaces mingle and blur and provide what life does not, and this is the space where all art exists, and all magic, and I would argue as well, all love."

> "And that's why I've chosen to write these pages as I've written them. For only by stepping into the middle zone, the polychrome edge between truth and untruth, is it tolerable to be here and writing this at all."

The overall impression given by these discussion points is that they represent a very close reading by the preparers of the questions, and these points also establish how important a close reading of the books by group members is for producing the most rewarding discussion session possible. Discussion of either or both of these two books, centered in the points proffered here, can only result in a rich, deeply involving, and considerable probing of what the books accomplish.

Even if a potential reader-discussion leader is looking over the questions without having yet read the book(s), it would be obvious that surface-skimming has no place in the discussion "program"; that sober, probing reflection on what the book's pages hold will be necessary before the discussion events.

I have to say that these questions are some of the most intelligent, most creative, most relevant, and most discussion-inducing I have ever seen. Regard them closely, for your own purposes.

And now let me go into the questions more specifically, to see what we can learn about their effectiveness.

The most impressive aspect about the questions concerning Doris Kearns Goodwin's *The Bully Pulpit* is how often and well they bring the material in the book into today's world. Let's face it, Teddy Roosevelt, William Taft (particularly he), and the muckraking persons of the Progressive Era could easily remain, in most readers' eyes and caring, in the world of long-gone and remote. But questions such as questions one, two, four, and nine pull these past events and trends into contemporary times, making the reader/discusser draw parallels between then and now, and in the process taking the reader into the pages of the book to comfortably appreciate Roosevelt's and Taft's experiences.

Question three is important, and a good conversation starter. With the book's focus especially on the two presidents—both men, of course—it is vital to totally understand the times and for seeing how completely Goodwin covers her subject so that her illumination of the women in the story is strong, especially in bringing to the fore the important roles played the two First Ladies, Nellie Taft and Edith Roosevelt.

Question seven is an excellent approach to discussing Goodwin's skills as a writer, and question eight brings the reader deeply into the book, asking what at first may seem like incidental questions that aren't directly related to the book. But this sequence of questions gathered into question eight will not only readily involve readers but also spark answers that will circle around and be very germane to the book. Thus, to me, question eight is a perfect point of discussion about a nonfiction book. The ensuing discussion will undoubtedly be rich and rewarding, as would the discussions emanating from question eleven, which is all about reader/discusser participation in the book.

Tartt's *The Goldfinch*

The overall tone of the questions about Donna Tartt's magnificent novel *The Goldfinch* seems to be more elevated than that which emanated from the questions about *The Bully Pulpit*, and that is almost inevitable. The discussion of fiction automatically exists on a higher plane if you are discussing a novel of the caliber of *The Goldfinch*, because you are broaching the realm of literary criticism, which is beyond casual, over-the-back-fence conversation about a less-than-literary novel that centers on such points as "How did you like it?" and "What did you like about it?" I'm especially referring to question 11. A discussion point like this is definitely for a reading group that is well-read and articulate. This question could definitely stifle conversation, and so it is thoughtful that it was placed last, after which more readily embraceable discussion points have been posed and given responses to.

The opening question is quite provocative. Art and artifacts that are lost are a blow to civilization, which is also due to a terrorist explosion. As this question indicates, loss is a major theme in this novel, and considerable areas of the novel can be opened up by discussing that thematic element in *The Goldfinch*.

Question three allows a group discussion of the novel's structure. The problem cited in the question was a real issue in reviews upon the book's publication, and structure is a greatly important aspect of a novel—and should be held up for group discussion.

Question seven centers on an important issue for appraising any novel: How tightly does the plot of a novel need to be tied to time and place? Will references to the cultural furnishings of a time period date a novel, or make it authentic? Does it boil down to the number of cultural artifacts cited? If it has too many and the novel dates too quickly is it not possible for it to achieve the status of a classic?

As I've briefly indicated, the subject of style is the most personal of the aspects of fiction—in terms of reader appeal, that is. Question nine addresses this issue. I particularly appreciate the way this question approaches style. Rather than simply asking if you liked it or not, the question presumes you would like Tartt's writing style if you are an appreciator of vivid, even beautiful, language. And that is a safe, sound presumption. No one can deny Tartt's command of rich sentences. The question avoids some readers' estimation of "language" that is too vivid —"language" being used here pejoratively. The question does not suggest that non-appreciators are *wrong*, but it moves directly to the generally highly regarded beauty of Tartt's prose, which any lover of "language"–used positively this time—will applaud.

EXAMPLES OF QUESTIONS TO ASK

These questions are not presented for exact duplication. They, of course, would make no sense applied to any other book. I offer them as inspiration for arriving at probing questions on your own that relate directly to the book under discussion, instead of just cookie-cutter, generic questions that can be used as a template for *any* book discussion.

APPEAL TO EVERYONE

A perennial issue for librarians organizing book clubs is how to attract male readers to your club. That problem stems basically from the fact—problem?—that most readers are women and certainly most public library users are women, and consequently, while most book clubs don't necessarily cater to women, they seem to attract more women than men. What to do about that?

Books are bait. Lure men into your group as you would lure that largemouth bass with something too attractive to his eyes and stomach to resist. Start a mystery book club. Men love mysteries, but don't choose Miss Marple-type cozies, instead, lean toward the hard-boiled school of detective fiction. (Don't worry, a lot of women mystery lovers appreciate hard-boiled thrillers, and frankly, if they don't precisely appreciate that school at the outset, they will quickly come around. After all, women are much more ecumenical readers than men; they will "experiment" more readily and bring into their reading realm books of a type or on a subject they heretofore didn't identify with.)

If you are forming a "regular" book group—meaning, you plan to have your group read books on a range of topics and consequently you will not be selecting exclusively from a certain niche, then male readers can be attracted by the promise of plenty of nonfiction—since the majority of fiction readers are women—and, specifically, history and biography should be well-represented on your reading list. The Civil War, the two world wars, naval battles—all these topics will make good bait. And, besides, most women—most women who are good readers, that is—will enjoy these books, too. Remember, women are more open about their reading material. After all, they agree that readers can *indeed* learn something from a novel!

My Bibliography of Good Books for Group Discussion

What follows is an annotated bibliography of 18 books that I deem good book discussion choices. Remember, book clubs are not given over entirely to fiction; nonfiction titles should be on every book club's agenda (unless it's a nonfiction niche group, and we've discussed that). This bibliography is based on my sentiment that women can, and will, read almost anything of outstanding quality; but there are "finds" in here for male readers as well.

(These titles are listed here in random order.)

The Great Railway Bazaar, by Paul Theroux. 1975.

This contemporary classic of travel literature reads as crisp and relevant as it did when first published. Theroux's account of riding trains as many times as he could in Asia puts more vivid emphasis on the people he met than on the places he saw. Rich in characterization, like a good novel.

Born Round: A Story of Family, Food and a Ferocious Appetite, by Frank Bruni. 2009.

It is ironic that Bruni, former restaurant critic for the *New York Times,* has all his life struggled with an addiction to food. His honest memoir is at once poignant and humorous, and completely enjoyable throughout.

The Joy Luck Club, by Amy Tan. 1989.

With particular appeal to the women in your book club, Tan's novel, the first of a series of books she has written about her Chinese heritage, tells the heartfelt story of four Chinese women who formed a support group in 1949 in San Francisco. Alternating chapters give voice to the women and their daughters, which, fitting into a larger picture, gives voice to one aspect of the immigrant experience in America.

The Fire Next Time, by James Baldwin. 1963.

This distinguished novelist (*Go Tell It on the Mountain* and *Another Country,* among others) who passed away in 1997, will be remembered primarily for this masterpiece of combined reviews and essays. Through his personal experiences growing up in Harlem, and his personal encounters with Nation of Islam leader

Elijah Muhammad in Chicago, Baldwin presents a searing indictment of American racial injustice.

All the Light We Cannot See, by Anthony Doerr. 2014.
Winner of the Pulitzer Prize and the Andrew Carnegie Medal for Excellence in Fiction, this is an illuminating, enveloping historical novel about the lives of a French girl, in self-imposed exile with her father in the French city of Saint-Malo from occupied Paris during WWII, and a young German soldier, sent to the same city to unearth local spies against the Third Reich. For people who value a compelling writer's voice, this is a special read.

Double Indemnity, by James M. Cain. 1943.
Believe it or not, I would nominate this novel as a candidate for "The Great American Novel." *Double Indemnity* is all about sheerness: ordinary vocabulary couched in simple sentences nevertheless minutely evokes a dark mood of immense sadness, in 1940s Los Angeles. An insurance agent is lured into a housewife's plan to murder her husband. Reading this, you wonder why any novel needs to be more than 100 pages long!

Cold Mountain, by Charles Frazier. 1997.
Frazier's first novel changed the literary landscape: before *Cold Mountain*, historical novels were usually considered genre fiction that serious fiction writers would not deal with, but after *Cold Mountain's* publication, which garnered wide critical response and more than one literary award, historical fiction was taken seriously. This Civil War novel follows Confederate soldier Inman from his wounding in battle to his walk back to his home in North Carolina and his great love, Ada. Loads of rich detail.

Cleopatra: A Life, by Stacy Schiff. 2011.
Schiff astutely, even beautifully, cuts through the myths and misconceptions surrounding the life of the legendary Egyptian queen. The picture created of Cleopatra's capital city of Alexandria is complete and indelible, as is the author's re-creation of the ancient world in which Cleopatra was a primary character. *All history appreciators will fall headfirst into this biography.*

Madame Bovary, by Gustave Flaubert. 1856.

If you want to proffer your reading group a timeless classic, *Madame Bovary* is as classic as they come. Flaubert's carefully composed story—every word meticulously paid attention to by the author's sharp eye and ear—of the frustrated wife of a French provincial doctor and the trouble her suppression leads to has captivated readers since its publication. Surprisingly modern in style, though.

The Great Gatsby, by F. Scott Fitzgerald. 1925.

In any reader's and critic's estimation, this is *the* "Great American Novel," by one of the best twentieth-century American writers. Fitzgerald's tale of 1920s high life is seen through the prism of the escapades of fabulously wealthy Jay Gatsby and his pursuit of the married Daisy Buchanan on New York's Long Island. Precise plotting matches immaculately conceived characterizations.

Stories I Only Tell My Friends, by Rob Lowe. 2011.

If you have a book group interested in adding a celebrity memoir to their reading list—and a responsible one at that—then this is your ticket. Lowe has been in the acting business since he was young and his look back over his career, particularly the people who populated it and lent their impression to it, is charming and honest. He's more than simply a pretty face, and his book will not put off serious readers.

The Guns of August, by Barbara W. Tuchman. 1962.

The opulent Edwardian Era, with its country house parties and crowned heads swaggering across their little kingdoms and principalities, came crashing down in 1914 with the advent of World War I. Historian Tuchman's very detailed account of the first 30 days of hostilities that were a harbinger of the pointless destruction that constituted the following four years of the war is a classic of military history.

Five Days at Memorial: Life and Death in a Storm-Ravaged Hospital, by Sheri Fink. 2013.

Top-grade journalism is practiced in this revealing, riveting chronicle of events during Hurricane Katrina and the immediate aftermath of the intense flooding as it was experienced at New Orleans Memorial Hospital. This is a stunning depiction of disorder in the face of natural forces and human crises.

Death of a Salesman, by Arthur Miller. 1949.

Miller, one of the twentieth-century America's foremost playwrights, created a lasting character in Willy Loman, to whom we can all relate as a consummate tragic hero, who dreams big and fails big. With interesting supporting characters, the play will live on and on as a stirring depiction of one great American story.

Killer Joe, by Tracy Letts. 1993.

This is the first play written by the hot contemporary playwright Letts, author of *August: Osage County*. The Smith family conspires to kill the mother for her insurance money, and they hire Joe Cooper, police detective and part-time contract killer, to do the job. Complicated mayhem ensues in this shocking depiction of one family's dysfunction.

Rabbit, Run, by John Updike. 1960.

The late Updike is considered one of the foremost fiction writers of the twentieth and twenty-first centuries, and the novel that put him on the critical and popular map was *Run, Rabbit*, the first of his quartet of Rabbit novels, featuring the life of Harry "Rabbit" Angstrom, whose life and career is a personalization of the hopes of small-town America hoping to live out the American dream.

This Is How You Lose Her, by Junot Diaz. 2012.

Diaz is hot news these days and rightly so. His most recent fiction is a series of interconnected short stories limning the "love" experiences of Yunior, a Dominican immigrant to New York. Through him the reader is exposed to a wealth of arresting characters, all bound by the vicissitudes of love; and it is the voice that holds readers: Yunoir's street-smart, idiom-filled, rough, but at the same time tender voice, which remains ringing in the reader's ears long after the book is finished.

A Moveable Feast, by Ernest Hemingway. 1964.

Hemingway, of course, is noted for his fiction; classic novels like *The Sun Also Rises* are seen as partners in effectiveness with his moving short stories. However, my favorite Hemingway book is this memoir of his life in Paris in the 1920s as a member of the so-called Lost Generation. He rubbed shoulders with Gertrude Stein and Scott Fitzgerald; in those days he was young and innocent, which is the charm of the book. Readers who enjoyed Woody Allen's movie *A Night in Paris* will relish it.

NOTE

1. Hilary Mantel, *Bring Up the Bodies,* (New York: Picador-Macmillan, 2013), 95.

Chapter Four

When Authors Speak

We continue to move up to the next rung on the ladder of the librarian's involvement in book and author programs. In this chapter, we will address the situation of inviting a single person into your library, either that person being an author who will speak about herself or himself and, as is usually the case, will read from his or her work; or that person being an expert on an author and will share with a public library audience his or her critical thoughts about the author being focused on this particular program.

Both situations require investigation and initiative. Searches will be necessary. Expenses need to be considered. Advertising is crucial. (You simply *can't* have an empty auditorium when you have invited a guest speaker to come speak.) But now you can really show your mettle as a book-and-author programmer. No, certainly, you are not the only one on stage (except, undoubtedly, when you are introducing your speaker), but the behind-the-scenes work has been done by you and fellow staff members and volunteers, and—this is important—everyone who attends, including the author himself, will understand all the work that went into this event long before the author stepped to the microphone. No, you don't want to brag; yes, you do want your efforts recognized.

So, just what are these efforts? Let's explore them.

Local Appeal

I would say that the first time you the librarian want to put together an author event, start small. Don't go for a giant like Alice Munro or, even in this day of his intense popularity, Anthony Doerr. Find a relatively local author; but, of course, the requirement is that he or she be a published author, even though what I'm about to say could arouse controversy and disapproval, I will say it anyway. Your attempt to attract a writer to come to your library should be focused not on a self-published writer but on one who has been published by a recognized publisher. After all, you want to attract a crowd; if it is a book with limited release, and has been self-published, chances are it will not have a big draw. Here's a hard—harsh, in other words—fact: self-publication does not carry the cachė with the general reading public as publication by a recognized book publisher. It boils down to the question of vetting: a book published by a reputable publisher has been vetted by editors and marketing people who have agreed the manuscript is worth the expense of publication. Something self-published has not passed through such scrutiny, and there is no guarantee that a self-published book has gone through the traditional methods of copy editing, fact-checking, and proofreading.

But at the same time, in the absence of huge name recognition, it's best to find someone who will have some local appeal. Your library is in a midsized city in central Illinois. Go with a writer who has written a novel published by, say, a university press (which translates in the public's mind as excellent credentials—which it is!) that is set somewhere in the region, and based on your personal opinion, publisher publicity, and reviews (you are never absolved from having read the book and found it interestingly linked to your community, and if it's gotten reviewed, having taken into consideration other's opinions, and weighing any negative comments before deciding on this book and this author), you have discovered a thematic and situational circumstance in the novel that you are certain will connect with an audience drawn from the community. Let's say your library is in a big city in the Southwest. A large metropolitan area promises richer author pickings, a wider range of subject appeal, and a stronger number of writers to select from. A nonfiction author resident in your part of the Southwest could have written about history, religion, geography, culture, and many other aspects of southwestern life and any of these specific areas would have an appeal and thus create an audience.

Your publicity for this event would emphasize that this author is someone that you, the reading public, should know, and this author has written a book that you should know about. In other words, you don't advertise the author as someone your prospective audience probably never heard of but someone you should know. Publicity, of course, always stresses the positive. (And more about publicity for your event in a later chapter.)

Big-Name Author

There will come a time, then, after the introductory experience of sponsoring author events that feature not especially well-known authors, when you feel ready and confident to graduate to an author of big-house rank, and by that I mean a writer enjoying name recognition outside a specific geographical region, and who has been published by a major publishing house. ("Big-name" is a relative term, of course. Alice Munro, Richard Ford, and Doris Kearns Goodwin would be top-rank these days, but with Munro's compromised health and considerable renown after her Nobel Prize win, and with Ford's and Goodwin's active writing lives, they are simply off limits. When I say big-name, I don't necessarily mean first echelon. Second echelon is more suitable.)

First, I would say the bigger the name, the less chance you will have in obtaining her or his presence. The bigger the author, the more invitations she or he has in their pocket, and consequently that writer's schedule is already crowded. Second, aim for someone who is popular with the reading public, especially someone popular in your library. How about Jodi Picoult or Stewart O'Nan? Good, solid, well-recognized names, that is. For nonfiction, consider the likes of Jon Meacham, author of well-regarded biographies *Thomas Jefferson* (2012), and *American Lion* (2008) about Andrew Jackson; or Sebastian Junger, author of *The Perfect Storm* and adventure author par excellence. (Later in this chapter, I will offer the names of several more writers in this category.)

You could always try to attract the most recent winner of the Pulitzer Prize, the National Book Award, the National Book Critics' Circle Award, or the Carnegie Medals for Excellence in Fiction and Nonfiction. These winners are always of great quality but are not always very famous. Of course, in the wake of their recent wins, they may be heavily booked. Or they may have decided the need to charge big bucks to make an appearance. But look over the list of past winners for ideas for an author to invite to your library.

You Get What You Pay For

Going hand in hand with the decision of how big a name you are interested in and will seek as a speaker—and consequently how far and wide you are willing to search for one—is the very important issue of expenses. Are you willing to pay an honorarium and transportation costs to and from your library, if necessary, and overnight accommodations and meals, if such expenses prove to be a requirement for the particular author whose presence you'd like to secure? Have *no* money? Your options are limited, then, of course. But not hopeless. After all, librarians are famously creative for doing lots of activities with meager funds.

Let's start with the barest of situations, then: no money to offer, or at most only a small honorarium of say, $100 or $200, which hopefully won't—and probably wouldn't—break your programmatic budget line. Obviously, you are going to have to cast your net close to home. Well, on second thought, that is not *too* obvious a statement; an author living some distance away, even far enough for you to need to buy a plane ticket or pay for gas mileage, may agree to pay his or her own way if the right button is pushed. That "right" button is, of course, the *library* button. *Libraries are valued cultural institutions; they do good for the community*—this is the script I'm giving you to send to an invited author—*and so coming to speak at my library would be a generous act on a humanitarian level. And good for you on a practical level. You will attract book lovers, your dream audience. You will spread word of yourself and your writing. That can only help to increase book sales. Everyone knows that librarians are perpetually short of money. It's a sad truth. What do you think? Would you be available and of a mind to come without financial backing from us?*

You—you the librarian now, of course, and I'm "off script" at this point—could make an effort to compromise. You could propose that no speaker fee would be offered nor transportation costs, but you would pay for an overnight stay. Don't beg, but don't hesitate to be honest about what your financial limits are. And always say a word or two about what a good cause it is. Because it *is!*

But as I've said, it pays to start small and local. Start with an author who is close at hand and inexpensive, and in that way you can build an audience for your author programs. In the process, generating high-level publicity and more intense interest, and perhaps establish the framework for starting a fund to which corporate backers or just personal borrowers contribute, all for the good of the library and thus the community.

Space for Your Author Program

Early in your planning for an author to speak or to read from his or her work, you will need to think about space issues. Just how much space do you have? Sufficient only for a small group? Accommodations for a much larger one?

There is an inherent contradiction in my advice about space because there is an inherent contradiction in the whole public program space issue. Previously, I'd admonished you—the librarian—to start small when planning to have an author come speak. But a small-potatoes author, so you are thinking, won't fill an auditorium. What if that is what you have for program in an auditorium that seats at least 500 people? The more people who have heard of your author, the more people will be interested in seeing her or him, hearing her speak, and getting his autograph (a program element I will address in a few pages). It's a truism to be counted on. Also, a truism is that there are few things more disappointing to a speaker than looking out over an audience and seeing only a few pockets of people here and there and plenty of vacant seats in between.

I still say "start small." But make a wise decision as to whom you invite. Remember when I said it would be productive to get a relatively local person who has written a novel or collection of short stories or something with thematic linkage to your community: say, stories that depict rural and farm life in the Midwest, and that environment is exactly what surrounds your town or city and the nature of that existence is understandable to your library patrons; or a novel that probes academe and its peculiar environment and you have a college or university in your town. Or a relatively local person who has written a nonfiction book about a feature or factor in your community that residents can relate to and would appreciate learning about: say, your library is in tornado alley and someone nearby has written an account of a recent, particularly destructive tornado that wreaked havoc close to where you are, or any kind of natural disaster that has lived on in local history; or your library is in St. Louis County and an author who resides there has published a guide to local festivities and attractions and historic places.

And then what do you do? You promote the heck out of your upcoming author appearance. Obviously, your publicity can't rest on the big name of the author. It will rest on those connections to interested prospective audiences, like the ones I've suggested above, which will establish a connection between the author and your community. You will probably make it clear that hearing what the author has to say will make you, as an audience member, wiser, and more aware of a book that it would be a shame to miss. Direct personal appeal must compensate for lack of wide name recognition if you want to fill the seats in your meeting place.

Authors Talking about Authors

Speaking of being wise, it might be wise for me to state in no uncertain terms the basic premise of this chapter, which is: You can and should, on a somewhat regular basis, get an author to come to your library to speak about his or her work and read from it (or just the latter, as many authors may prefer to do, supporting the principle of "let my work speak for itself"). Or you can get an author who has written about another author, and most commonly that would be a biography covering a writer's life, and you can suggest he or she discuss the subject of his or her book and the process for writing it. Thus, here are the two options we are concerned with in this chapter.

We have already addressed the first option. And let me remind you that at the end of this chapter I will supply a list of authors I have found suitable for such an engagement. But now, let's turn our attention to securing the appearance of an author who will come speak about another author. Sound strange? Not at all. Writers frequently study the life and work of another author, usually a relatively major one, usually now deceased. (For instance, as I am writing this, I have novelist and biographer Jay Parini's biography of novelist Gore Vidal, *Empire of Self*, waiting on my desk for review.)

So, let's deconstruct the situation as it relates to inviting someone as speaker. You have author "A," who may or may not have extensive credentials in his or her own right, but acceptable enough credentials for a recognized publisher to have signed this person on to compose a study of writer "B." That study may take the form of a biography, with minimal space given over to criticizing (in a literary "criticism" way) B's work; or, at the opposite end of the spectrum, it may heavily emphasize literary criticism, with biographical material more like the mayonnaise holding the tuna together rather than being a "flavor statement" all on its own. Most often, it's a 50–50 or 40–60 combination of the two.

I advise that you as the organizing librarian be prepared; and by that I mean if you are interested in having as a speaker an author who has written a book about another author, get your hands on the book or at least read a lot in terms of the author you are attempting to secure as a speaker. But—is this a warning I'm issuing or simply a suggestion I'm offering?—at the same time, go for a big subject. What I say is this: small author, big subject. You want to draw an audience. A small author talking about another small author may not do the trick. Small author discussing a big author, with good promotion behind the event, emphasizing the name recognition of and the appeal of the subject, will bring interested readers in.

Naturally, the perfect "storm," as it were, would be a big author talking about another big author. Reasons for why that is an excellent situation to bring in a large attendance are obvious.

Where to Find Authors

You as a public librarian are professionally connected, aren't you? Can you really be doing your job well if you are not networking, at least on a small scale? Let's assume you have established communication of some nature with the public librarians in your immediate area, through a professional association that is either informal or that has some set proceedings. If your library is part of an established system or cooperative, you have connections right there.

So, the first step is discovering what authors are out there and available, and, importantly, if they are open-personality types who will deliver a good presentation and not be the introverted-writerly types who struggle to even make eye contact—oh, how uncomfortable that is for the audience that you've made such a great effort to attract—is ask around your network for suggestions. Deciding who to invite should be based on a librarian's experience, and, as I've said, it is equally important to decide who *not* to invite based on the not-so-good experiences of the librarians you've contacted.

At this point, may I suggest that if your area's librarians do not already have an online database that can be shared (not with the public, of course), then it would be a wise idea for you to start one. Such a collection of information takes the form of a directory of authors in your region, and includes: up-to-date author contact information; the speaker fees the authors are known to charge; the categories in which they write; the titles of books and articles they've written; and comments from librarians who have had the experience of "employing" that person as part of an author event. The latter is important, for you want this to be kind of an Angie's List, so librarians will not only learn about the authors in their region and if they write material relevant to your library community, but also so librarians can discover if other librarian's opinions generally go against an author as a possible participant in an effective and even enjoyable author event. This directory would need to be maintained regularly—meaning, updated frequently with new and revised information—if it is to be always useful.

A division of the American Library Association called United for Libraries has as its own mission to be a national network of library supporters, including library trustees, library advocates, and "Friends of the Library," and their advocacy extends from local to state to national levels. One of the United for Libraries' initiatives is a project called Authors for Libraries, which can be reached at www .authorsforlibaries.org, and its purpose is to connect authors with libraries. Just exactly what we're talking about! Authors join online (for a fee) with a credit card or print out and fill in a paper form and mail it back with a check; librarians can join United for Libraries and then have access to this important directory, which is greatly helpful in locating and securing the services of an author in your area. (Librarians can search the website by Zip code.)

The Authors for Libraries website has a fact sheet on booking an author for one's library; it is rich in helpful, ever-important information for securing an author for all kinds of library programs and events, and that fact sheet will be relevant to all the author events I will be discussing. Put a sticky note on this page so you can refer to the URL at any time, with no need to turn pages to find it.

There are two suggestions I want to call out, from all the thoughtful suggestions this fact sheet provides. The first is suggestion number two: plan in advance. A six-month lead time is recommended before you contact an author or an author's people. Use this time to get settled exactly what kind of event you want and what exactly you want from an author. And the other suggestion I want to do a shout-out over is suggestion four, specifically the second part, which reads this way: "Get in touch with the publisher to get an author's booking agent for best-selling and highly popular authors." Sage advice.

Along those lines, the Michigan Center for the Book has placed in the public domain a sample contract between a library and an author and a sample memo of understanding between the library and the author, which spells out all necessary details for the commitment. Find both at www.michigan.gov/libraryof michigan/0,2351,7-160-54574_36788_38908-102310-,00.html.

Special Requirements

It is wise to immediately establish, right after securing your author, what the author's speaker requirements are, especially concerning any special equipment requests, such as a projector or a VCR. It has been my experience that author readings and signings do not require much more in the way of basic equipment than the library would automatically provide to begin with. But, needless to say, it is best to know in advance.

What Do You Want Me to Do?

Once you are in contact with a potential author/speaker, or that author's publicity manager at their publishing house, make it clear to him or her in no uncertain terms what you would like the events to entail. It has been my experience that most authors want that kind of direction and specificity; they generally don't want it to be said to them, "Oh, do anything you desire." Unless the author or his or her representative indicates to you early in your phone or e-mail communication that they have what I call a "stump speech"—like a politician's stump speech, which is a prepared address delivered more-or-less verbatim on repeated occasions—then they customarily will turn to you for instructions on what you would like for them to do for you.

Give the author a time frame. I would suggest an hour and a half to two hours. Just an hour and your audience may feel cheated out of a good program; longer, and they will perhaps grow restless. For the author, two hours also is a good time limit. If you ask for much more time, he or she may feel they have an inadequate amount of material for filling up that mount of time. Of course, let's face it, authors tend *not* to have timid demeanors, tend *not* to be not interested in talking about themselves. Yes, there are exceptions; no law says you can't be shy and introverted and be a writer. But I bring this up as a "warning" about the time length of his or her talk and/or reading. An author may agree to between an hour and a half and two hours but once started, he or she might be having such an enjoyable time that the 90 minutes have come and gone. What to do? You as the coordinator/moderator decide. If you are paying her for an hour's work and you suspect she might end up arguing for "overtime," then give her or him the throat-slash sign that universally means "wrap it up."

I would suggest that before the author takes the podium, you say privately to him or her, "If you want to keep track of time and don't want to be repeatedly checking your watch, look to me every once in a while and I'll give you a sign at the fifty-minute mark, in case you want to end exactly on the sixty-minute point and then wrap it up." The reaction will give you a good clue as to his or her intention of following direction or being loosey-goosey about time constraints.

I have to say, though, that I cannot imagine, really, an author who speaks or reads beyond the agreed-upon time and consequently requests more money from you, unless you have on your hands a mega-important writer who, because their time has become precious, calculates every second "working" as "paid working." Again, talk about it beforehand, in this case long beforehand; and if the author is that big, you undoubtedly will be dealing with a representative, and may even have a publisher contract to sign. But the flat-fee issue should be addressed—politely—so there are no surprises after the event itself.

Here is my bottom-line sentiment about all this: If the author is a good reader and/or speaker and you have gotten a good sense that the audience has warmed to him or her, *let the author go!* Let him or her take all the time they want. It's a once-in-a-lifetime experience for you and the audience to see and hear this author, and you want it to be as remarkable and memorable as possible.

Split the Time

I would suggest that *you* suggest to your author a "split" time: half to share details about their work habits, research requirements for what they have written, why they write what they write, etc.; and half the time to read from their work. If they simply read for the full time, I guarantee the audience will begin squirming. And even the author may perhaps grow weary of such a reading length.

Years and years ago, I attended a reading by the great American novelist (now deceased) Saul Bellow, who read from what I consider to be his best novel, *Hum-*

boldt's Gift. It was a program consisting of him simply reading, with no "speech" before or after or even a question and answer session afterward. He read for nearly two hours. In the evening! After everyone presumably had eaten dinner! I admire Bellow and his work immensely. But I grew droopy-eyed. Occupy that length of time with nothing but reading, and what have you? No connection was established between the author and the audience. It might have been someone else reading from the pages of *Humboldt's Gift.* With no context having been established by Bellow, and no preliminary "one-on-one" with the audience to give background to his writing this particular novel, you received no personal connection for having come out on a winter evening to lay eyes on a major writer.

To add insult to injury, he was a bad reader. Monotonous, with no crack of a smile nor any eye contact with the audience. He seemed to have never read *Humboldt's Gift* before; I mean, as if he were reading someone else's work. His pauses weren't for effect; they gave the impression of lack of familiarity with the words in front of him!

Question and Answer Sessions

I do not know if most readers enjoy Q and A session at the end of their program, but I do know that most expect it to happen.

It's best to factor in a question and answer session into the hour-long program; and inform your author that he or she should expect it. It has been my experience to leave about ten minutes at the end of the author's reading for Q and A; again, inform your author of this plan. Ten minutes is a good "core" time; if you have a reticent audience and the Q and A fizzles, ten minutes is not a long time to call the program over. On the other hand, if your audience is eager to engage your author, a lot of exchange can be packed into ten minutes; and if the enthusiastic Q and A spills over the hour, let it go! Who will mind? Nobody gets tired of an exciting Q and A. My experience informs me that most audiences at any author event will state almost unequivocally that at least half of the information they took away from the event, and at least half of their enjoyment of it, in watching and hearing the author, comes for the Q and A. Why is that? Because by way of asking questions, the audience tailors the event to their interests and "needs." The audience can "personalize" the author's presentation by connecting what *they* want to know in addition to what the author has already told them.

But, don't *let* the Q and A session fizzle! It's more or less your responsibility as event organizer, presenter, and moderator to keep it alive. In other words, a "dry" audience should not be allowed to kill the final minutes of an event, because it risks leaving a bad taste being in the audience's mouth that will taint their impression of the whole event. What if the audience is "dry" right off the bat, meaning few of them are brave enough to be the first to stand up, walk to the microphone, and talk in front of everyone, and are especially uneasy talking in front of the quest speaker? Don't simply throw up your hands and say to the crowd, "OK, thanks for coming."

Come to the event with your homework done; and homework not only means a prepared biographical introduction to the author but also a set of "starter" questions. Or "seed" questions, if you will. These will be, more or less, your insurance against a dead audience. I would suggest having at least three questions prepared, focusing on some aspect of the author that *you* would like to know; and a good question that will connect the speaker to your audience is to ask about the formative influence of libraries—public or school—on his or he life goals and professional accomplishments.

But in arming yourself with questions that hopefully will stimulate the audience to follow suit, *flexibility* is the key word for describing how you should proceed. By that I mean that you may have a set of good questions that you created the evening before the program, but you have to pay attention to your speaker—of course you would—and to the words he or she has said, determine whether these words are read as part of the book he or she is reading from or are off-the-cuff personal remarks about the composition of the work, etc. It makes for a much fresher, more relevant, more composed event if you ask a question about what has just been said. Of course, let the audience go first, if it's obvious that an audience member or several have a question just waiting to be asked. If the Q and A is off to a slow start, or—and this is important, too—if the Q and A slides to a stop after just a couple questions from the audience and you as moderator feel it's too premature to call the event over, then you should ask a good, "productive" question, a preplanned one that you feel is keyed to the author and his or her work after having heard their reading or talk, or you ask a new, unplanned question, one that you compose on the spot and that is keyed to something the author said or didn't say (and you desire the point to be further addressed). Just remember, keep the questions flexible and the Q and A going.

Long-Winded or Heckling Questions

It may seem rude or even unprofessional, but I say interrupt, politely, if a questioner falls immediately in love with the microphone and the sound of his or her voice (or the profundity of their own questions). After the passage of a sufficient amount of time for a succinct question to have been articulated, indicate, with a smile, that time is limited for the event and prompt that person to please ask the question forthwith so the author-guest will have time to offer an informed answer and, importantly, to answer other audience members' questions.

An even worse scenario occurs when someone in the audience takes the opportunity to essentially kidnap the microphone to air their sentiments on what the author has read or spoken about, or to try to set up an argument with the speaker, or even worse, to take off on some tangent that has little or nothing to do with the author or the author's book. This is an obvious no-no. It can ruin the event. You as moderator have an obligation to nip this situation in the bud. *Interrupt,* I say again. Interrupt by asking the person if they have a question, and if not, please give the microphone up to someone who does.

Obviously, you've made arrangements for some sort of security for your event, especially if it's at night; and this is when you will be glad you have someone on hand who can be called on to escort the person out if the situation deteriorates to that degree. But think positively: long-windedness often happens, and it is just a nuisance; heckling is rare, a threatening atmosphere even rarer.

Publicity

Publicity is basic and essential for the success of your author event. Like any book program, this author visit needs to be brought to the attention of not only your library patrons but also the general public, and spread as widely as possible. Or, guess what? Scant attendance. Word gets around among authors; they may hear, or they may ask, what your attendance has been on previous author visits. If your event has a pattern of "modest" turnout, it may become increasingly difficult to attract an author, especially if you are seeking one with a "name."

Regardless of your willingness to pay a speaker's fee, authors don't want to speak—or read—to empty chairs. No speaker's fee, when you've secured the services of a top-drawer author who will amuse/entertain, inform, and even energize a small group—such that their enthusiasm will fill the room—can make up for a sparse audience. The event is likely to be joyless from start to finish.

Where to Focus Your Publicity

My list of places to submit publicity information should come as no surprise to librarians who have been involved in public programs. The places of course include:

1. First and foremost, announce your author event, *any kind* of author program, on your website, just as you would any upcoming event in your library (except, give this one an extra push—meaning, write it up as the *major* event of the season);

2. Ask the author's publicist to participate in promoting the event, in venues they are accustomed to employing, which may stretch beyond your thinking or budgeting;

3. Prepare a press release to send to local media, including newspapers and radio and television stations, and if there is a college or university in your town, contact the college newspaper editorial staff for announcement space in their publication that they can let you have for free;

4. Take advantage of online calendars maintained by city government, for local civil and social events the general public might like to know about;

5. Prepare posters to be affixed to library doors, both external and internal; and ask local bookstores (if there are any!) for permission to use some of their window space for a poster;

6. Bookmarks with upcoming library events slipped into books at the circulation desk; and the frontline staff working at reference and circulation desks to verbally remind patrons of the upcoming author event;

7. If you have obtained funding for the event from outside your library, ask the funding agency if they require that information about them be included on every publicity piece;

8. If your library has a newsletter, then, of course, this is a perfect place to announce the upcoming author appearance; and, as in all release of information, make certain details are correct: proofread, and proofread again;

9. Senior citizen and retirement facilities make excellent places to post information about the event; and perhaps you could even talk with the activities director about providing bus service to and from the event.

A Book Discussion

Here's an interesting idea: How about hosting a book discussion group in advance of the author's visit? Of course, it will be a discussion about one of the author's books (or about the author's only book, if that may be the case) and, if the author has written more than one, the discussion should be about the book the author is going to read from and/or discuss. Preliminary discussion with the author via e-mail will reveal which book that happens to be. You may need to specifically ask, and you can state your reason for asking, that you want to conduct a discussion group about the book shortly before the event takes place. What author wouldn't be pleased to learn that? I can't imagine an author being reluctant to divulge such information. Besides, the title of the book to be focused on would be a good fact to include in your publicity for the event.

Autographing Sessions

It will be expected by the author and the audience to have an opportunity for the author to sign copies of the book that was discussed and read from.

The cardinal rule to remember is to not have the author handle any commercial transactions. You will want him or her to focus exclusively on verbal exchanges with "customers" and signing the book. And don't expect the author to bring books to sell (unless they are published by a company that does no marketing and sales and simply dumps multiple copies into the author's hands, for him or her to sell on their own; this usually means the author has already bought them at a discount and will sell at full price and thus the difference between the two will be the author's profit). Or the author may make this sort of arrangement on his or her own, which means the author, on his or her own initiative, buys many copies, using the author discount, and thus voluntarily carts them from signing to signing, keeping the money, of course—after all, all those copies are his or hers to do what he or she wants to do with them.

These are questions you need to ask yourself if you are planning an autographing session.

1. Where in the auditorium—or whatever room you have designated as the speaker venue—will a signing table fit? Indeed, it will be necessary to have a table upon which copies of the book will be stacked and for the author to sit at; but also acceptable is a room or hallway close to the reading area, where the author can adjourn. Make certain you announce at the end of the reading where exactly audience members should go to purchase a book and have it signed; and make certain you have figured out beforehand the logistics of where the line of book buyers should "snake" and thus be orderly in the waiting line. If you just let people flock to the autographing session, a small mess will likely ensue as people who join the line won't be certain if they are standing at the end or in the middle. Have a library staff person indicate where the line should go, based on your pre-planning. A traffic coordinator, if you will.

2. Where are your books coming from? If the author is taking care of bringing materials, so be it. If not, then you basically have two choices for securing copies for the author to sign. The publisher can provide them or your local bookstore. (Need I state that the details of this need to be ironed out very soon after signing your author for a reading and signing?) Other details that need specifying early in your planning stage include: who is playing "bookstore clerk?" If the library is responsible for making the sales, have a staff member or a Friend of the Library do the job. If the publisher has sent copies, arrange beforehand what is to happen with unsold copies; returned to the publisher, yes, but at whose expense?

Other Details to Contemplate and Resolve

1. Are you interested in a printed program for the audience? I stand on the side of having a printed program being a good idea—a *classy* idea. It can be as uncomplicated, as unfancy, as you want; but make certain the date, the location and the guest speaker are indicated (and particularly make sure the name is spelled correctly; proofreading is an essential in planning and executing an author event). And handing them out at the door is a special touch, more personal than simply leaving them on seats.

2. Library staff will need to be involved in your author event, and standing at the door passing out programs is an important task that a staff member must be efficient and friendly at.

3. Other staff members will need to "float" around the auditorium, or whatever the speaking venue is, to answer questions, but more importantly, to give the audience the assurance that this is a tightly run, efficient, professional, and thoughtful program geared to making the audience comfortable and informed.

4. You, the event organizer and, expectedly, the event introducer and Q and A moderator, will need to: be free to greet the guest author and, if there are any people accompanying him or her, greet them as well; have a "greenroom" prepared, where you and the speaker and his or her "people" can come together and greet each other; and get to know one another to a basic degree, so that everyone will be made more comfortable. If you do all these things, I guarantee the event will run more smoothly and be more personal. In the greenroom, have coffee, bottles of water, and a tray of fruit; and let the speaker know there will be a bottle of water on the podium as well.

5. Confirmation between you and the speaker should have occurred at least the day before the events, and directions to the library, including parking information, should be provided.

6. Would you be interested in taking the speaker and his "entourage" to dinner before the event? I believe the right thing to do is make the offer. If taken up on the invitation, invite your staff who will be involved in helping out with the event, the library director (if that is someone other than yourself), and the president of your library board. The author won't be intimidated; he or she will be flattered.

7. If the speaker is flying in, meet her at the airport, and of course have a hotel room reserved for her. Either you or a staff member should accompany the author to the reservation desk, to make certain the reservation has been kept and the bill will be sent to the library and not handed to the author the following morning at checkout time with the expectation of immediate payment. I was once invited to do a program at a public library, and we had no time—the two sponsoring librarians and me, having to go directly from the airport to the restaurant—to permit me to check into the hotel before dinner. After dinner, I was dropped at the door, and at the check-in desk I learned my reservation had been cancelled because of an incoming convention taking precedence over

little ol' me. What was I supposed to do? I asked the desk clerk. Well, this hotel had a branch at the airport and someone would drive me out there. I had my program to give early the next morning and I made them promise I would be brought back into town in time. Everything worked out, but you don't want your author feeling stranded like I did. Confirm the hotel reservation 24 hours in advance; if it's been cancelled, then obviously you need to find accommodations for your author elsewhere.

8. A nice gift, nothing extravagant or showy or obviously ridiculously expensive, is a cordial idea. Present it quietly; do not make a production of it in front of the audience.

9. Some physical "evidence" of the event should remain beyond the event itself. If nothing else, have a staff member or staff member's spouse or your spouse bring a camera for shots of the speaker and other participants (shot before or after, certainly not during!). A tape recording of the whole event will be nice for the archives or even to borrow by interested patrons. (Of course, make copies; some copies loaned out may have a way of *not* being returned!) Videotaping will be the best choice. But make certain you have clearance from the author to do so. And speaking of photographs, hire a professional if you have the money. It will pay off.

10. An audience evaluation form should be included in the program you pass out, and once they have been filled out, attendees should place them in a box at the door as they are leaving. It would be helpful to pass out pencils before the event begins. Make your evaluation questions basic, such as: What did you especially like about the event? Any dislikes? Have you attended other programs in this library? Would you return to another author event?

11. Have a staff member count heads. Knowing how many people attended your event will be helpful for additional funding, submitting reports to the board and to the city government, and securing authors in the future. And for your own personal satisfaction, of course.

Possible Authors to Invite

As I've said before, start small. Invite local talent. A highly enjoyable event will certainly be the result. And if you feel that the theme of your whole series of author events is to support and sponsor local authors, I say hats off to you. The local public library should be on the vanguard of supporting the local arts and literary scene.

If, however, you decide to go "bigger" and want to invite an author with national standing, go for it. Remember, the biggest authors in the land may be too big a trophy for you and your means, but what follows is an annotated listing of authors with recognizable names but who aren't giants. On the other hand, know for a fact that all these authors will put on a great—greatly informative and entertaining, that is—program.

These names listed here are in no particular order, just randomly presented:

William C. Davis

An American historian, professor of history at Virginia Tech and director of programs at that institution's Virginia Center for Civil War Studies. Twice nominated for the Pulitzer Prize, Davis had written more than 40 books on the Civil War and southern U.S. history; one of his most notable is *Crucible of Command: Ulysses S. Grant and Robert E. Lee: The War They Fought, the Peace They Forged* (2015). Davis is a good pick to attract a male audience.

Charles Frazier

He is famous for his first novel, *Cold Mountain* (1997), which was made into a successful movie and ushered in the current renaissance of historical fiction, which shows no signs of abating. *Cold Mountain* was the 1997 National Book Award winner. Frazier has written two subsequent novels, *Thirteen Moons* (2007) and *Nightwoods* (2011), but his name will forever be linked to his first one, a rigorously researched and dramatic narrative about the Civil War from a southern perspective.

Michael Chabon

A significant writer you would be pleased to have come speak: genial in personality, good with audiences, author of such high-literary but purposefully "popular" novels, including the highly praised and much-loved *The Amazing Adventures of Kavalier & Clay* (2000), which received the Pulitzer Prize. It is a historical novel covering 16 years in the lives of two cousins who created a very popular series of comic books in the pre-WWII 1940s. Chabon's first novel, *The Mysteries of Pittsburgh* (1988), was a best seller and brought him immediate fame. *Wonder Boys* was

Q&A

Kaite Mediator Stover is director of readers' services at Kansas City Public Library and a frequent program speaker at library conferences.

I know you have all kinds of book and author programs at Kansas City Public.

KCPL's author events fall into one of two categories. They are either public conversations or solo presentations. For public conversations, KCPL will try to find a local person with more than passing knowledge in the author's subject area. We encourage a casual give-and-take format designed to showcase the author's personality and/or expertise. The interviewer's role is to pull out the most interesting tidbits of an author's work, encourage the author to tell a story that is related to the work, help the audience get to know the author as a person. KCPL has used library staff in this role. I interviewed Mary Roach, Doug Dorst, and Caitlin Doughty. We have also used community folks. I interviewed Anne Thompson with a local film professor. My job was to keep the conversation from becoming too much "inside baseball." Mitch Brian's job was to make sure the conversation went below the surface.

When KCPL does solo presentations for author events, we very strongly encourage the author NOT to read from their work. We inform publicists and get in touch with authors to help craft the kind of program that will engage an interested audience and encourage them to purchase a book to further their knowledge. KCPL has learned that audiences appreciate background information on a book's topic that

might well have been excised from the final edition. KCPL audiences also respond well to visuals and digital slide presentations are encouraged. Authors are expected to talk for about 40–45 minutes with an additional 15 minutes for a Q&A session followed by a book signing.

What are some of the frequently encountered problems in getting programs like these organized and presented, especially when it comes to getting authors/speakers to agree to participate?

The biggest challenge libraries face in scheduling an author event is financial. There are travel and accommodation costs to consider and an honorarium. Some authors ask for speaking fees in the amount of $5,000 or more in addition to expenses. Scheduling dates that accommodate both author and library can also be a challenge. Followed by marketing and promotion to guarantee an audience that means a successful event.

How do you avoid common problems in book and author programs or solve them if they happen?

With sufficient planning most problems can be solved before they occur. Venue, equipment, content, book sales, can be handled days before the event. The point person for the event should make sure the author understands the size of the room and the number of attendees to be expected. Equipment should be tested the day before the event, without fail. I cannot stress that enough. Even if the library has used the equipment before. Test it the day before the event. Test it two hours before the event. If the author has a presentation get it in advance on a flash drive and test it. Unless it cannot be avoided, never let the author bring the presentation to the event at the last minute without time for testing. As least two weeks before the event, the organizer should get in touch with the author about the content of the event. Nothing should be a complete surprise to the event organizer nor the author. Book sales should be arranged at least one week before the event. Have a backup plan in case all the books sell out. What would you give an attendee who wasn't able to purchase a book and have it signed?

Issues at the event. Have an AV/tech person remain on-site for the presentation's duration. This person's sole job is to make sure the equipment is running properly. Check in with the bookseller and make sure the bookseller can take checks and credit cards.

The event host should be ready to handle the audience during the Q&A. Don't be afraid to announce "We have time for one more question and then Ms. DuMaurier will be signing books out in the lobby. If you didn't get to ask your question, perhaps there will be time during the book signing."

What have you learned not to attempt to do in this kind of program?

We have learned not to tie in too many activities in one night's event. We try to keep it simple and keep all the attention focused on the author. We try not to put additional people on the program or different topics that don't mesh with the scheduled author. We have learned not to leave anything to chance or the last minute. On the day of an event, the only thing library staff are concerned with is the number of attendees. Everything else is handled. We have learned to designate one person to be the point person who handles the speaker and off loads all other tasks onto staff. One person can't handle everything all at once and do it well.

◇◇◇◇◇◇◇◇◇◇◇◇◇◇◇◇◇◇◇◇◇◇◇◇◇◇◇◇◇◇◇◇◇◇◇◇◇

his second novel (1995), and it was made into a successful film version. Try to get him for an author event; he will put on a good show and attract a large audience.

John Green

His name is everywhere these days; he is an author of young adult fiction that has strong adult crossover appeal. His major novels thus far include *Looking for Alaska* (2006) and *The Fault in Our Stars* (2012), which debuted at number one on the *New York Times* best-seller list, and the 2014 film version opened at number one at the box office. He is often credited with a shift in YA literature to reflect real—that is, flawed—people. As big as he has become, he remains a friend of libraries, having worked as a publishing assistant at *Booklist* early in his career.

Tracy Chevalier

Anyone who has ever read a book has indeed heard about Tracy Chevalier, or at least heard of her most famous book, her second novel, *Girl with a Pearl Earring* (1999), which is, of course, based on the creation of Vermeer's famous painting with that title. She has written six other novels and is considered a foremost practitioner of historical fiction these days. Personal experience leads me to say she is a warm, engaging, articulate public speaker.

Jennifer Weiner

Weiner writes incomparable love stories, beloved by followers of so-called women's fiction. Her novels are always best sellers. A self-described feminist, Weiner has been quite outspoken against what she perceives as gender bias in the media: meaning, books by male authors are automatically reviewed as just as good as, if not better than, books by women. Her most famous novel probably is her first, *Good in Bed* (2001). As a featured writer at an author event, she will generate a good audience who will be very stimulated.

Marie Arana

Again, based on my personal experience, I can say with certainty that Arana is a well-poised, open, intelligent speaker and interviewee. Born in Peru, she served as the book critic for the *Washington Post* for more than a decade. Her first book was *American Chica: Two Worlds, One Childhood* (2001), a memoir about her bicultural childhood. Her most recent book is the very rigorously researched and fluidly presented biography *Bolívar: American Liberator*, about the George Washington of South America, Simón Bolívar. If you think your audience won't be interested in that historical figure, think again: Arana will capture the attention of all audiences, including male readers, with her talks and observations about this important figure in South American history.

Diana Gabaldon

Of course, this writer is nearly a cult figure for her *Outlander* series of novels, in which she dexterously and knowledgably mixes the genres of historical fiction, fantasy, romance, and mystery; a television adaptation (2014) has only increased her renown and popularity. Time travel is the basic conceit of the Outlander novels, set in a mid-eighteenth century Scotland during the turbulence created by the refusal of the supporters of the Stuart dynasty to sit back and see their native line of kings displaced by the German Hanoverians; and set, too, in the twentieth century, from which nurse Claire Randall travels back in time to the Stuart uprising days. Gabaldon is big-time, and snaring her for your library may not be easy, but if successful, it will certainly be worth with the effort.

Chapter Five

Author Interviews

In each chapter thus far, we have taken a step further up the ladder of the librarian's involvement in book programming and planning author events. The next important rung necessitates your complete participation, with the added "stress"—read "reward"—of doing it all in front of a live audience. I refer to interviews with authors—on stage, among an interested live audience. Now, of course, you as the coordinating librarian for book programs and author events can also turn the actual interviewing process over to someone else, someone on your staff eminently comfortable with stage performance, or even someone in the community who would enjoy performing the task and with whom you have advance confidence in their doing so. I retract the word "task," since the experience of talking books with an author is a thrill and a pleasure.

Underscoring my comments and suggestions that follow is the fact that an interview event need not be limited to one author. I have done author interview programs over the years that involved as many as four authors. I might add, and I would recommend, that four be the maximum number of participants you as the moderator should engage with; more than that and the event can get bulky and the panelists will spend too much time simply sitting and listening to the others and consequently you, as the program sponsor, won't get the bang for the buck that you would like to have realized.

In this chapter I will share my experiences and ideas concerning how to best interview an author; these are my suggested principles for interviewing one or more authors.

Who Does the Talking?

My fundamental philosophy in interviewing an author is that the audience—or listeners, if the interview is being done by webinar or other online vehicles—is "there" (meaning present and listening interestedly) to hear what the *author* has to say, *not* the interviewer. Well, certainly, the interviewer will be judged by the audience as to his or her effectiveness in drawing relevant and interesting points and even anecdotes from the author being interviewed; so what I'm saying is that the interviewee is not invisible, but is the vehicle by which the author communicates herself or himself. Nevertheless, the moderator's efforts should be subtle and unobtrusive, and in the process, not draw more attention to oneself and one's questions than to the author and his or her responses. Again I say, people don't come to hear *you!*

Control, Yes; Dominate, No

I once interviewed, for ALA's online (virtual) annual conference (the lunch-hour author interview that was presented on both days of the virtual conference), a famous historian, and one who enjoys a widespread following and critical esteem. Not some crusty, narrow, academic figure only über-serious listeners would be interested in, that is. Attendance was high. And the historian proved to be perfectly charming; he and I quickly established a rapport, and—I may say—by my perceptive questioning (it helps that I have a college background in European history) he responded with dynamic answers, broadcasting his great expertise and his book's multidimensional appeal. The half-hour interview ended before I knew it, and, honestly, I could have talked to him for much longer. In other words, I enjoyed the satisfaction of a job well done—and having established a communion with a major author.

Attendee comments were encouraged by the ALA organizer of the event. One comment directed to my author in particular snared my attention. A man wrote in to say, in an obviously vexed tone, that the author talked too much. He dominated the interview, said this man. And, of course, implied in his criticism was that I let my great historian run over me and run away with the interview.

This man's criticism aroused annoyance, of course, but it also aroused, in my defense (which I did not share with him but nevertheless formulated in my mind), thoughts about the most productive ways of conducting an interview; and those thoughts centered on my opinion that my interview with this historian had been conducted soundly. What I had done with him adhered to my first principal of interviewing, which I elucidated above: people aren't there to hear you, but they are there to hear the author. (Now, of course, the audience expects the moderator to set the context of the author and his work within a general picture of contemporary writing and to guide, by asking questions, the author into talking about, discussing, and revealing features and factors of her life and work.)

I liked to think that I had chosen my questions wisely; having read the book closely and with great interest, I had a pretty sure sense of what specific topics within the large canvas of his book would have the most dramatic appeal to talk about. Of course, there never is sufficient time to explore with an author all the sub-topics he or she addresses in a nonfiction book. So, as in the case with this important and popular historian, I selected a few I believed would generate good discussion.

When reading a nonfiction book by the author you will be interviewing, be sensitive to the author's tone—or, more specifically, changes in the tone. It's been my experience as not only a reviewer but also an interviewer that close, careful, attentive reading will reveal the author's particular excitement about certain subtopics within the narrative as whole. It's like listening to someone talking and hearing them hit a subject they have a particular interest in, have special passion for; and the tone of voice will change—subtly, yes, but a heightened intensity will be detectable. Experience in detecting the heightened tone in written prose is the key here: experience on the part of the reader in being sensitive to the specific topics—which may be covered in only a few paragraphs—that the author has a keener interest in than the other areas of the bigger narrative. If you can develop sensitivity to these, and base your questioning on them, a well-above average, exciting, and informative interview will ensue.

Basically, what I'm saying is the author's interest in your questions will spark an enthusiastic answer and one that contributes to—no, is the "meat" of—a very engaging interview.

How to Begin

Still speaking here of interviewing the author of a nonfiction book, you begin by asking of the interviewee, "In just a couple sentences, tell us what your book is about." The author will pause, having sensed immediately that he or she can't simply open their mouth and let words just flow out; that, instead, they will have to formulate—quickly, and on their feet, as it were—a response that meets your request for brevity. But I also say this: this early in the interview let the author have her way. If the couple of sentences you asked for actually turn into ten sentences, don't interrupt. Save your interruptions for later, because, predictably, if an author finds trouble in containing himself right off the bat by limiting description of his book to two sentences, interruptions may indeed be necessary later on. But, remember, *only* if necessary. Remember what I said about people coming to the author event: their interest is in hearing what the author has to say and thus expecting the moderator's introduction and questions to be minimal, to only serve as the vehicle for the author to shine. Certainly, being an interruptive questioner at the outset will set the wrong tone, one that suggests you are perhaps combative, and that your control of the interview is more important to you than letting the author be herself and do what she should be doing—capturing all the entire audience's attention with her words.

Pay Attention!

Look at the author's lengthier description of her book (lengthier than you had asked for, that is) on the bright side, which introduces another important principle in interviewing an author. Yes, you have your prepared questions at hand, and a few extra ones in case the interviewee is rather clipped in his answers and you have more time to fill than what you had planned for; but the best interview is one in which the questions arise organically from the previous response by the interviewee. A dry, non-fluid interview is one in which the interviewer is more concerned with checking off his or her prepared questions than with "elevating" the interview into the realm of an actual discussion, with each participant—interviewer and interviewee—riffing off what was just said by the other person.

I know what it's like sitting in front of a large audience conducting an interview. After all, I have interviewed authors at ALA's Author Program held at every Midwinter Meeting, and the audience can reach up to a total of 700 attendees. You don't want to be looking at your notes while the author is answering a question to see what your next question is. The author will gather you are not really paying attention, and *his* interest level will shrink as a consequence. I say don't be locked in "preparation." Concentrate on what the author is actually saying, pull out an item the author has just mentioned, one that you feel would be interesting to the audience to see pursued further, and formulate your next question around that. It's called thinking on your feet—although you are actually sitting, of course. Posing a question that you just came up with doesn't mean that you can't go back to your "script" at any time, especially if you've prepared some questions you are certain will result in a productive, rewarding interview.

But, let's face it, the more attention paid to the author and the more your questions are tailored to his responses, the more comfortable—and, yes, flattered—he will feel, and a blossoming will likely happen right before your eyes.

Picking the Dramatic Moments

Another aspect of preparedness that can only pay good dividends when interviewing a nonfiction author is, while you are closely reading his book, to determine if this is an author you want to go out of your way for to have come to your library, then mark the dramatic moments in the book. Here is another suggestion/ rule of mine: select an author of *narrative* nonfiction. Not a book that is "just" factual. A book that has life and personality. A biography or memoir, or a science book about combatting new diseases, or geographical exploration, or a good history book. You get the picture; you know what narrative nonfiction is. Once you've read the book by your prospective invitee-interviewee, if you have found little forward movement or sluggish movement through the narrative, think again—about the author, I mean. I'd say if there isn't swift and compelling movement, then find another author to interview. Sluggish prose too often translates into a slow-going interview.

Back to my original point. In your careful reading, you will discern the rise and ebb of dramatic episodes, like the swelling and breaking of waves. That is the usual and positive rhythm of narrative nonfiction. For instance, in my interview for *Booklist* with popular historian Doris Kearns Goodwin, about her 2013 book *The Bully Pulpit* (in case you are not familiar with this spectacular book, it's about presidents Teddy Roosevelt and William Howard Taft and the Progressive movement in American society and politics and journalism during their terms in office), I asked Goodwin—by the way, an easy, comfortable person to speak with—to talk about one certain event, among the many, many events that filled her well-written pages, that she hadn't devoted considerable space to but never-theless had struck me when I read the book as a drama-filled episode bound to be interesting to an audience hearing about the book: that is, the assassination attempt on former President Roosevelt during the complicated three-way presi-dential election of 1912.

My experiences with recognizing and isolating particular stories and anec-dotes that I thought would eminently please an audience informed me to say to Goodwin, during the course of our interview, "Tell us about the assassination attempt on TR." She did so, and, as I had hoped for and expected from her, to great dramatic effect; and even though my interview was for print—to run, as I've indi-cated, in the pages of *Booklist*—I could easily imagine, as if I were actually "hear-ing" it, a live audience being drawn in closer to hear what she had to say. I knew I had scored an attention-grabbing moment.

These are what you seek as an interviewer: attention-grabbing moments, when the audience literally moves forward to hang on every word of the inter-viewee. Potential attention-grabbing moments are what you make notations for as you're reading the book. "Ask about this." "Ask about that." Avoid asking big, general questions that might lead the author to talk on and on for too long a time to keep the audience's rapt attention. In other words, don't ask, "So tell us about the Battle of Gettysburg." Ask, instead, about the effectiveness of a certain general or a troop movement in the battlefield. Or public reaction at the time to President Lincoln's speech dedicating the cemetery. The best interview puts together the bigger picture as if by assembling a mosaic. Each of the smaller pieces you ask about are themselves little dynamic, interesting, revealing pictures adding up to a bigger "mural."

Big Author

If you are fortunate enough and have sufficient financial resources for library programming to score a big author—one with a wide readership and thus exten-sive name recognition—then here are some "rules" I have established for myself and have continued to live by when I've interviewed the "biggies."

First of all, don't be all-fawning. Authors hate being fawned over. Most of them, anyway. If, on the other hand, you discover you have on your hands an author who seems to require being fawned over—by a detectible degree of condescension in their demeanor right off the bat and which doesn't seem to be dissipating after the first few minutes, or they were dropping hints early on about how good it was of them to have agreed to participate in this event—chances are you're dealing with an insecure ego and will have to tiptoe around his or her fragile sense of self, at least for the time being. But I insist that while you certainly need to be cordial and helpful and, yes, indicate your thankfulness for their agreeing to appear, don't give in to their insecurity and be "toady." Remember, as the old cliché goes, they put their pants on one leg at a time, too.

Secondly, don't ask obvious questions—more specifically, don't ask questions that have been asked of this author a million times. Now, if you haven't been following this author—"following" meaning paying attention in print or online to what the interviews with him or her have been like—then consult print or online sources to gain insight as to what he or she has been asked in previous interviews. Or, basically, just figure the situation out yourself. In other words, think about what would be the obvious and easiest questions that surely have been asked before and don't create your battery of questions based on these questions you sense have been part of every interviewer's "kit."

But let me issue a caveat: Don't necessarily chuck all the questions that you think have possibly been posed before. Feel free to ask a couple rather easy questions that you nevertheless feel really get to the heart of the book and the author's purpose and treatment. After all, some basic information about the book needs to be established right up front, and early in the interview no one will be thinking: "Seriously? That old question again?" Anyone in the audience who has a clear head on his shoulders will realize that certain "matters" about a book need to be established immediately.

For the rest of your interview, the "meat" of the interview, in other words—the part that distinguishes your interview from all others and what the audience will remember most about it—try to view the subject of the book from a slightly different angle, not head on. What I mean by that is, try to personalize the topic by isolating one individual who was involved in the story—a major player, to be sure—and asking the writer to fit that individual into the overall picture that the total book creates. Or dramatize the topic by asking the author to relate to the audience an episode you found particularly compelling.

Remember me talking about interviewing Doris Kearns Goodwin about her splendid book *The Bully Pulpit?* That was a good example of what I'm talking about: isolate and personalize. "One of the most interesting events in the whole book," said I, "is the attempt on Teddy Roosevelt's life. Tell us about that."

Another for-instance: I was honored to interview the 2013 winner of the Carnegie Medal for Outstanding Nonfiction, Timothy Egan, for his biography of photographer Edward Curtis, *Short Nights of the Shadow Catcher*. (I might add here that Goodwin's *The Bully Pulpit* also won the Carnegie Medal for Excellence in Nonfiction, the year after Egan won the award.) Curtis's masterpiece was the 20-volume *The North American Indian*, a photographic documentation of the customs of nearly 80 Native American tribes. One of my questions to Egan was: "One of the most interesting stories in your book is Curtis's investigation into what really happened at the Battle of Little Big Horn." Egan's immediate response: "I'm glad you picked up on that, because Curtis doesn't get the credit due him." Egan went on to provide a full, rich, explanation of Curtis's proof of General Custer's cowardice.

Remember, too, that I said it takes some practice to come up with the attention-grabbing moments? Let me add this to that: When you are reading a book by an author you are interested in asking to come to participate in an event in your library, read it with the audience in mind. What aspects of the book do you think *they* would like to hear about? Balance that with the aspects of the book that *you* personally would like to hear about, would like to know more about. How did I know to ask Timothy Egan that particular question about General Custer? One, it was a piece of the story that held particular fascination for me, so my motive in asking had a selfish element to it. But only partly so. In reading this marvelously informative book, I discovered, upon reading the Custer episode, that here was a name and an event—the Battle of Little Big Horn, that is—that certainly the majority of good readers would have heard of. Click! It was the best connection between the interview listeners and the book. A bridge for them to enter into and at the same time an "excuse" for whom I had immediately recognized as an articulate— but at the same time unpretentious author— to wax eloquent on a topic I was guessing he would enjoy sharing with me, the interviewer, but on a greater scale, all the readers of the interview as well. And I hit the jackpot!

Fiction Writers

As far as I'm concerned, what I have to say about interviewing fiction writers applies to big and small: that is, local writers with limited name recognition or, on the other hand, one of whom everyone in the reading community will have heard of.

Like nonfiction writers, writers of fiction see through gush to the artificiality with which it is presented. Don't gush over them; don't act as if fiction writing is next to godliness (even if you feel that is so!). As it does with a nonfiction writer, fawning makes the author and everyone within earshot ill at ease and self-conscious. Act normally! Peer to peer, even if you have Donna Tartt in your library, ready to be interviewed by you or someone on your staff.

As when interviewing a nonfiction writer, when interviewing a fiction writer avoid any questions that are likely to have been asked before—especially questions you have guessed have been repeatedly asked. Again, don't face the author's work head on; approach from a side angle. Even if his or her book is—or books *are*—novels. After you've asked the author to summarize in two or three sentences what his or her book is about, then ask how she or he sees how the story she has created in her novel demonstrates issues we all face in the contemporary world, or if the novel is set in the past, even in the recent past, how does the author's historical setting have parallels to today's world. In other words, after a brief exploration of what the novel is about, then approach it from an oblique angle, which will be the best approach for letting the author give his or work relevance to everyone in the audience. I guarantee the resulting connection between the writer and the audience will be palpable.

Let's move on to the subject of character. "Your main character is thus-and-so." (A sentence identification will suffice.) "Tell us how in your mind you conceived and developed him into the character you would have him to be—or, if you believe that once created, characters take on a life of their own, then how you let this character go in the direction he wanted to go in."

Next, if the novel is historical, "What is it about this time and place that interests you?" (Now, this question may have been asked of him before, but it's worth asking anew, because as you see it fits well into the sequence of questions you are posing.)

The next step will be to identify the novel's theme as you see it, and ask the author to conform or adjust your theme identity to closer suit his own idea. And then ask, "Are novels built around that theme of particular interest to you?"

If the author is male and some of his characters are female, ask about the difficulties of an author inhabiting the psyche of the opposite gender—an especially interesting question if the main character is gender opposite to the author.

You can go on from there. I think you have a good idea by now of how to make the interview your own. Tailor it to your own style and to your audience: the key to successful interviewing.

If I may throw this in: Don't conduct interviews on the level of Ellen DeGeneres. She's a warmhearted, likable, generous person, and her afternoon show is meant to entertain and not provoke much thought and introspection on the part of her audience. But, still, the superficiality of her interview questions is often quite astonishing. If you haven't watched her show, do so for a couple episodes and you'll see what I mean. You'll want your audience to come away from your interview with an author a little wiser about the writing process and a little more familiar with the author as a person.

Watch the Clock

Have someone watch the clock for you; if your interview is billed as a half hour, then it should last a half hour but not much longer than a couple minutes over. Your clock-watcher should alert you, by some prearranged sign, when you've five minutes left, so you can wind things up, and then again when your time is up. If and when you are given the five-minute warning, and if you're in the middle of a question, go ahead and finish it and let the author answer you fully. If you've just completed a question and answer sequence, ask a brief final question that you know will spark a brief answer.

— *Chapter Six* —

Panel Discussions

Panels, panels, panels. Library book programs and author events are all about panels; a majority of book programs and events relating to books and authors are presented in the form of a panel, which, as most people realize (I'm not sharing private information here, in other words!), is a grouping of like-minded individuals, or individuals who actually may not necessarily be *like*-minded but have some sort of connection through the work they do. Anywhere from three to a half-dozen is the usual number (any more than that would be too cumbersome to be effective), all of these panelists sitting at a table or dais, as it is properly called, in front of the curious faces of an audience who came to hear what the panelists have to say. And, usually, the panelists, one at a time, give individual talks on a certain designated topic, each panelist contributing his or her personal expertise or opinions or experiences toward, hopefully, a full and comprehensive picture of this predesignated topic.

So, the librarian who is organizing a panel, or both arranging it and in turn functioning as moderator at the actual event, has a major concern right off the bat: how to compose a panel that will fall into a cohesive whole—an organized unit like a colony of cells—and not simply four, five, or six disparate talks that ostensibly "belong" together by theme or subject but have no real connection with one another other than being delivered at the same time on the same day at the same event.

However, let me remind you of something I said two paragraphs ago: A thematic or subject connection is pretty mandatory in a panel, but opposing views of that theme or subject is just fine. In fact, disagreement adds to the interest of the panel, and adds more personal appeal to a wider range of audience members. After all, not every audience member is going to share the same view as every other audience member, nor share the same view as each of the panelists.

As long as you keep arguments from breaking out. More about that later.

But of course, injecting that kind of life into a panel is not solely the product of good, wise panel selection but also of moderating the panel in such an effective manner that the best qualities of the panelists—that is, their expertise (why they are on your panel in the first place)—will shine forth.

How to compose, how to moderate. We will look at suggestions for and conclusions about those twin topics.

From Several Angles

I had previously advised that when interviewing an author whom you know has been interviewed many times before coming to your library for yet another interview, to avoid asking questions you could pretty well be certain the author has answered before—if not several times before; and my advice centered on "going at" the author's book *not* head on but from a "side" angle. I say that again when deciding who to ask to be on your panel. Approach the theme of the panel, or its subject, from the top, bottom, left, and right, and consequently give that theme or topic a multidimensional airing that will please your audience by allowing them to learn as much as possible about the book and issues at hand.

When choosing a topic for a panel, I would suggest thinking seriously before composing and conducting a panel on the three subjects that traditionally have been listed as "steer clear of" at all family gatherings: politics, religion, and sex. What I'm saying is: know what you're doing before presenting a panel on very controversial topics. An argument about Islam may stir anger among the panelists and even between the panelists and the audience. (Remember Ben Affleck's apoplectic appearance on Bill Maher's *Real Time* talk show in October 2014 when the subject "talked" about was indeed that?) Hot political issues might best be left to be debated when actual political candidates come face to face; and a "discussion" of abortion and homosexuality just might explode.

Yes, librarians are great supporters of free speech and unfettered access to information. But in composing an author event, what you don't want to have to think about is a fight between panelists and audience. Or disruptions within the meeting space or demonstrations outside. I say, it's not worth it. Bottom line is know your audience, which means in this case, know your community, which will inform you of what your audience will be. And while you don't necessarily have to play it safe, at least play it wise. You want to sponsor an enlightening book program without any risk of it descending into animosity. I'm just saying.

Now, let me backtrack a few minutes—a few pages—and talk about how, in the first place, to select a topic or theme. Praise to you if you've gotten four mature authors who have nonfiction books out on topics that are clearly allied, or three, four, or five novelists whose novels can be grouped together with sense and no strain. Panels may come with readily identifiable threads that are nice and strong. Perhaps you are "putting on" a panel of staff librarians, for the public or for other librarians in your system or both, discussing books newly accessioned into the collection. The only issue, then, is determining how many books each panelist will discuss and making certain there is no overlap among what books panelists will discuss. The connection between each panelist—the theme of the panel, that is—is readily apparent. Easy as pie.

I recommend making your theme as general as possible. I'd go so far as to suggest that it makes more sense, and makes things easier for you the organizer, if you line up a complement of authors or speakers or whatever will compose your panel *first*, and then, if they happened to have written—generally—about the same thing, then their common topic is both the panel's topic and its theme. "Four authors will come together to discuss various aspects of the conservation movement in the U.S." Easy as pie.

My feeling is, and I've been given two, three, and four disparate writers *many* times before, that you can always find a linkage, one that "justifies" (to the audience, at least, and really, that is all that matters) the panel and makes it seem that you already had the connection in mind when you gathered your panel members in the first place.

Examples

Let's say you have the opportunity to secure the speaking talents of two novelists who've written novels about "life" in contemporary America. As far as you can see when you are considering which one or both to invite to your library, there is not much more connection between the two than, as I said previously, "life" in contemporary America. I say, go ahead; book them both, even if they are not "huge" names. Trust me: You can make a good panel out of two authors, even if their commonality is as vague as life in contemporary America.

What the event will really be is a dual interview, but you bill it as a panel discussion. And you, as moderator, will have to realize that you will be more deeply involved in the discussion than if you were moderating a panel of four, five, six individuals—working with only two panelists requires your closer involvement—but you have great possibilities, then, for making strong, compelling connections between the two women's novels, for making the program "yours" in terms of the direction in which the conversation can go (and with just you and two panelists, the event will be very much like a conversation, which is all to the good).

For example, the author forum of 2012, which that year, as every year, *Booklist* and ALA's Conference Services and Exhibits Round Table put together every ALA Midwinter, and which for several years I served as moderator, was fortunate to snare two outstanding novelists, Hillary Jordan and Helen Schulman, who'd both written provocative novels recently, *When She Woke* and *This Beautiful Life*, respectively. I said to the folks at Conference Services, "Let's stop at two." I'd read both novels and knew I could make an interesting event with just the two writers. I saw right away what the connection would be.

Jordan's novel is a distinctive dystopian novel set in the near future; the premise being that convicted felons are no longer imprisoned with rehabilitation being the objective. Now, in the days in which this novel is set, felons are "chromed," their skin genetically altered to match the level of crime for which they have been convicted. The protagonist, Hannah, is convicted of murder, and her skin is tinted red, which will last until her sentence is completed. With "shades" of Hawthorne's *The Scarlet Letter*, Hannah must function in society as best she can, given her crime is apparent to all. The novel involves an array of social issues relevant today as well as the tomorrow in which the novel takes place, including, murder, abortion, and the dissolution of the separation of church and state.

Helen Schulman addresses the very current issue of sexting in her novel *This Beautiful Life*. The Bergamots did indeed have a beautiful life until one night when the 15-year-old son in the family receives and forwards a sexually explicit video of an underage girl. As quick as a flash, the whole family is turned upside down.

Immediately after reading both novels, I certainly saw how the two books could be connected by discussions about contemporary social and crime issues, but a stronger connection leapt out at me: these novels are about "shaming"—social ostracization that has been the theme of not only *The Scarlet Letter* but also Shirley Jackson's timeless and breathtaking short story "The Lottery," which, since its first appearance in the *New Yorker* in 1948, has been anthologized almost everywhere. And, sure enough, the overarching theme of shaming provided great grist for a discussion.

How to Moderate a Panel

Successful moderating is more than simply sitting at the dais with your panel and, in turn, introducing them, for each to give a 10-to-15-minute speech; and then at the end, asking the audience if anyone has any questions. Boring moderating often begets a boring panel. No matter how good the individual speakers are, how much they touch and enliven the audience, the panel will not be the well-remembered force that it can be if the moderator isn't running the show and drawing the panelists together and spurring them on to become the most involved and enlivening speakers they can possible be.

So, what are the principals of good moderating? Let's explore.

SUPPRESS YOUR NERVES

As I remarked in my chapter on basic principles of public speaking, the old adage that to calm yourself before a crowd, imagine them all in their underwear. It doesn't work, it's only a distraction, and the point of it is to reduce the audience in your mind from this big monolithic entity that's out to, if not see you fail, at least see what you're made of. I say allow your nerves to be at the surface of your moderating for a couple minutes. Nerves are like bacteria: they can't thrive but only a short time when exposed to open air. Even more so, pretend right before you joined your panel on stage you took an antibiotic. In the words of the Head of Infectious Diseases at Northwestern Hospital, bacteria are "wimps, and once the meds confront them, they run."

Your nerves are wimpy, too. After a couple minutes of dry mouth and a strain in your voice, the antibiotics—in this case, your realization that you are doing fine, will take over and you are free of nerves, and now you can sit back and relax and see that you are in command of the "show" and the dying nerves are being replaced by a growing confidence that you are drawing this panel into a force to be reckoned with.

FRIENDLY, CHATTY

Come to the dais with a smile. Maintain a friendly demeanor throughout, but don't project an artificial grin, because that makes you look smug and un-genuine. This sounds elementary, but the default expression for too many people is a frown, and if you know that to be the case with yourself, fight against your perpetual frown for this occasion and let people at least *think* you are having a good time and you are pleased they turned out for this event.

Speak slowly. Don't rush. On your notes or script, have "Slow Down!" written at least once per page as a reminder to yourself, to help protect against rushing and building up too fast a speed through your text.

Look at the audience as much as you can; establish eye contact, and that means not looking out above the audience to the back to the room, but, rather, look at individual audience members directly—for just a few brief seconds, because you don't want them to feel uncomfortable, as if they were being singled out for some reason.

TELL THEM WHAT TO TALK ABOUT

So, you've put together a panel based on a common element, whether "new fiction for the fall," or "SARS, now Ebola," or "Your book was made into a movie." The thread will be established for the audience by you in your introductory remarks and will be reinforced by what you've instructed the panel members—well in advance, of course—to focus their presentations on: their personal reactions to the theme of the panel.

And there I must be emphatic: no matter how "big" the names are on your panels, you as moderator must give them clear, precise directions beforehand—*weeks* beforehand—to what you want from them and expect from them. The truth is, panelists will appreciate the direction. If one resents it, then his or her "waywardness" will be obvious to the audience and will reflect badly on her or him, not you. You want your panel to appreciate and observe your direction.

I witnessed a panel at ALA made up of very distinguished Chicago authors, who individually were entertaining, but obviously the organizer/moderator had not attempted any pre-panel guidance (apparently she found herself intimidated by their fame), and the panel emerged with no real point, developed no direction, became pretty much a free-for-all for each author, as if they'd been asked simply to come and talk about whatever he or she wanted to talk about.

That can work at a certain level if you do have high-interest, high-profile panelists, such that people can walk away saying, "Oh, I came to hear Such-and-So and his talk was informative and, so, I'm satisfied." But they got very little from the panel as a whole, carrying very little away in terms of a bigger picture of the theme or subject matter.

THEY DIDN'T COME TO HEAR YOU

As I've previously indicated, the theme/point/purpose of the panel should be closely elucidated for the audience by the moderator in introductory comments. *But don't do the panelists' work for them!* Tell your panelists what to talk about, in advance, and let them do it. Don't, when "setting the stage" for them, completely cover their topic yourself. The audience did not come to hear you. Remember that. The moderator is the mortar. The panelists represent the bricks. People came to see and hear the bricks. Twenty-five minutes of introduction? The audience has lost interest in your introduction within five minutes, I guarantee it.

I summarize: Don't be so intimidated by your panelists that you are afraid to tell them, in advance of the panel, what you'd like for them to talk about. And, then, let them talk. Remember, you as moderator/introducer are—a food analogy this time!—a dollop of mayonnaise, and the panelists (the tuna) need only a small amount to make a sandwich that stays together.

ASK AT LEAST ONE QUESTION IN COMMON

I recommend that you begin each panelist's talk with a short—*short*—biographical introduction; and, now, if you've organized your panel to be a series of independent, discrete talks that cover different aspects of the major topic or theme, once you've introduced the panelists individually, your job is temporarily finished—until it's time to introduce the next panelist. Now, this is, of course, the "easy" way out for a panel moderator; you have only basic work to do. But what you gain in effortlessness on your part you lose in control of the panel's direction: control of the direction the panel is taking, control of "shaping" each panelist's contribution to the good of the panel and the panel's ultimate goal and purpose. What I mean by that is this: the best panel organization and presentation is a discussion format with you as discussion leader.

How that format plays out is this; and the best "physical" arrangement of the moderator and panel is that which the Conference Services department at the ALA devised for their big, mega, huge-audience-drawing Author Forums given just prior to the opening of exhibits at each ALA Midwinter Conference. The stage is dominated by five big, comfy chairs in a soft semicircle. The moderator sits in the center chair, the four panelists—two on each side of the moderator— range out beside the moderator. No one stands to deliver their comments; every- one—including the moderator—who is also the introducer, of course—remains seated during the entire program. That means, of course, there is no freestanding microphone. The moderator and the panelists wear a lapel microphone.

In this format, it is best for the moderator to introduce the panelists at the beginning. "On my far left is. . . . on my immediate left is. . . ." And so on. And in that same order, you the moderator ask the panelists a series of questions relevant to the topic (which means, of course, considerable preparation in advance). Keep track of time, of course; unless a certain panelist is given to pretty much "yes" and "no" answers (and that has indeed happened to me), you want to give equal time to each panelist.

And speaking of "equal." I always like to start my one-on-one conversation by asking the same questions of each panelist: in some fashion, I ask them to connect themselves and their work to the theme or subject of the panel. You don't want the audience—nor the panelists, either, of course—to perceive differing levels of "difficult" in the questions to which they are being "subjected"; you want to start things out on an obvious level playing field, which will go a long way towards put- ting everyone at ease.

Important in this format is for the moderator to be attentive and flexible. Because the good moderator is one that, yes, has done his homework and prepa- ration and has come to the event with sufficient questions to give good "airtime" to each panelist and to make certain the promised length of the event is fulfilled; but at the same time, the good moderator tailors his or her questions on the spot:

reconfiguring, if necessary, each question around the interviewee's response to the previous question.

I promise you that this will make a much more satisfying panel—for you, for the audience, for the panelists themselves—than one in which each panelist pops up, talks and sits down again; followed by the other panelist doing the very same thing. We've all seen those panels.

KNOW THEIR WORK AND PAY ATTENTION

Don't rely on the clichéd opening questions, "Tell us about your book" without immediately following up with additional questions going somewhat into detail about the book, showing the author and audience that *you* know *exactly* what the book is about because you read it carefully. And that is because you *did* read it carefully. If you've invited an author to talk about his latest book, know it well; know it backwards and forwards. Not to show off to the audience, per se, but to give the audience confidence that your discussion will be based on specific knowledge of the book and not simply superficial generalities about "that type" of book.

If you've invited an author to talk about the body of his work, then you are obliged to read everything in his oeuvre. Perhaps you won't have a specific discussion about a certain book, but you don't want a scenario where something about a previous book comes up in the author's remarks and all you have to offer is a blank stare; and neither do you want to be asked a question that, had you been familiar with the author's previous works, you wouldn't be sounding so peculiarly uninformed at best and simply silly at worst.

A good example of superficial questioning is that which is practiced by Ellen DeGeneres in her daily afternoon talk show. Now, of course, she is a kind, generous, funny person who is a major advocate of personal acceptance of race, creed, gender, or sexual orientation. Granted, she does not intend to be a scholarly, deeply searching interviewer with forceful instincts to get at the heart of a celebrity like no other interviewer has done before. Of course not; she is all about afternoon entertainment. Yes, too, she is not interviewing Nobel laureates but often just an ordinary, unknown person who has done something very humanitarily worthwhile; and when she has a more distinguished guest—a celebrity in the arts—you can see the "lameness" of her questioning: easy questions, puff-piece questions, questions more to flatter than elicit good information. It makes good TV. Not an especially good book-and-author event, though.

DON'T BE OVERLY CRITICAL

On the other hand, don't feel it is your obligation as moderator to "nail" everyone or anyone on your panel. A panel discussion is not a contest between you and the panelists; you are not out to prove you know more than everyone on your panel, or to prove anyone wrong with what they say. If that is why you invited a certain panelist, to show him or her up, shame on you. What I'm saying all goes back to my insistence that the audience didn't come to hear you. Also, if a panelist's books or articles have sparked controversy out amongst the reading public, it's not your place to debate him or her. Your place is to say, "You have aroused some disagreement among some of your readers. If you don't mind, tell us about the controversy." But for goodness sake, *you* stay out of the debate—meaning, keep your opinions to yourself. In essence, what I'm saying is, you have no business criticizing a panelist's choice of subject matter, questioning their expertise, or defaming their novels; your job is to present before the audience what it is that the particular panelist is good at and known for, without, of course, fawning over or overpraising them. You are a facilitator, not an investigator. If there is to be disagreement, and depending on the topic there may well be, then let it be between two or all of your panelists; and even then you are under an obligation to exert your implied powers as moderator to defuse any out-and-out arguments. Many in the audience would like to see that happen—a big argument, that is. But most would not, nor would you.

KEEP A SENSE OF HUMOR

Going hand in hand with keeping the peace is maintaining a sense of humor. Now, I don't mean that slapstick comedy should prevail; even the most entertaining panel members want to ultimately be taken seriously. On the other hand, a panel on a very serious subject doesn't preclude an occasional piece of humor—after all, no book program or author event taking place in your library needs to be excruciatingly painful in its attempt at seriousness. In fact, I would even suggest not inviting an author who has written a book about a bloody true-crime or any homicide death—meaning, if the death and the means of it is what the book is about, what most of its pages are devoted to, remember that you want your program to be enlightening but also entertaining; bringing an audience "down" is not to be commended. That might engender such a lasting negative response that people might never return for more of your author programs.

Keeping a sense of humor in this context does not mean giving yourself over to wisecracking. It means being flexible, and reacting with a smile to any mechanical problem with microphones or projectors, a recalcitrant panelist, an overly aggressive audience member when asking a question, or two panelists entangling their antlers. Don't reprimand or complain or otherwise let anger or even annoyance show. For mechanical problems, have someone attending from your library who knows mikes. If a panelist says only "yes" and "no," do not comment on his or her shyness or whatever is causing his lack of full participation in the panel's dialogue—just cheerily move onto the next panelist or next question or topics. To an aggressive audience member, say "I'm certainly pleased our panel has stirred passions, now we need to move on"—with a smile, of course.

PAY ATTENTION, MAINTAIN EYE CONTACT

We've all seen moderators and interviewers do this: pay more attention to their notes, to their watch or the clock, and stare out into the audience rather than focus on the face and words of the panelist who is currently speaking. In a word, don't. Keep your attention on your panelist. Don't look distracted; don't look as if you are not being drawn into the panelist's ideas. Certainly don't let your eyes go from face to face up and down the audience, as if you were taking the audience's temperature. To your panelists, that looks as if you are seeking the audience's approval, and like you are more interested in your approval rating with the audience than you are in what your panelists are saying and sharing. And if the format of your panel is indeed interview-type rather than single-presentation one at a time, then you want to carry on a conversation with the individual—which, of course, means looking at him or her.

In-House Book Discussions for Staff Training

Lucy Lockley is the collection development manager for the St. Charles City-County Library District in St. Peters, Missouri. Lucy coordinates the selection of all material for the adult collection; she personally selects all the adult fiction and has staff members across her library district select nonfiction from reviews in the review journals.

Lucy not only reads books but also orders books; but her book involvement does not stop there. She also *talks* about books. Organizing book discussions are an important component of her job, and Lucy has been nothing if not creative in devising a readers' advisory training program for the staff of her library district. "The program uses a combined book discussion and book talking format and covers multiple genres."[1]

Lucy does a yearly round that is comprised of 13 areas of fiction and then separate sections on nonfiction topics. Each year—for each round—a guest speaker is invited to the system to lead two workshops for the staff on one specific genre of fiction or one specific reader's advisory technique.

But Lucy also organizes a monthly Readers' Advisory Team (called the RAT Team, as Lucy affectionately refers to it, and refers to herself, as the leader, as the RAT Queen!). The routine is as follows: the team spends two meetings on each fiction genre or nonfiction topic. One meeting is a broad discussion meeting, in which everyone has already read and now discusses the same book; the second meeting is a book talk meeting, during which each participant talks about an individually selected title, so, consequently, everyone is reading two titles within each genre.

Let's return to Lucy's guest speaker initiative that I mentioned previously. I am pleased to say that I was a participant. In October 2011, Lucy brought me down to the St. Charles system to run two workshops on historical fiction: the agenda being that I would do one workshop on the afternoon of the morning I flew from Chicago to St. Louis and then do the same thing, but with another group of people, the following morning. I credit myself with being an expert on historical fiction, as does Lucy (which is why she asked me to lead her workshops, obviously). The workshops were to be identical, but as I learned, when audience participation is involved—is an integral part of the program—the plan you follow as moderator will be different each time, even if you arrive at the same destination each time, which, of course, is what is hoped and strived for. It was a meaningful experience for me as a book program participant—not as the organizer this time—to understand how to deal with an audience on a very personal, intimate level.

First of all, I previously mentioned that the good organizer (good as in making certain the moderator—if the moderator is a different person than the organizer) lets speakers and/or panelists know well beforehand what they should talk about; that is, the theme of the program and what the moderator hopes will be certain topics in common (of course, that includes topics on each panelist's personal experiences and philosophies). Lucy did just that: weeks before I was to travel to

St. Louis, she gave me a list of topics that her guest speakers on genre fiction traditionally cover, and which she feels are the topics that librarians in her system want to hear and learn about from guest speakers. But what Lucy *also* did, which is what a good organizer should also do, is give me lots of leeway in how to present my takes on the basic topics she would like to see covered, and these included the definition of historical fiction, my personal relationship to the genre, the widespread appeal of historical fiction (not its appeal just to me, in other words), readers' advisory in historical fiction, and good reads.

A workshop being a workshop, I certainly didn't want to stand and lecture for three hours, the length of each session. So I spoke not exactly extemporaneously but with notes before me, as loosely tethered to these notes as I could be and still have certainty that I included all the points I intended to include. The benefit of doing the workshop twice was that by the second go-around I've realized, based on audience response and reaction or lack of response and reaction, what pieces you have affixed to the general skeleton as outlined by Lucy work best and which ones do not work so successfully. And adjustments can be made. And in each session, I had to set aside some of my material because the audience wanted to talk about something else. I let them talk. And I learned from them. Bottom line, that is the wonderful aspect of leading a staff discussion among librarians you work with: the give and take. They learned, as I did; they revised their views on certain topics and books, as did I.

Lucy's program is a paradigm for staff instruction on books and authors.

NOTE

1. Rebecca Vnuk, "Notes from the Field: Everything's Up to Date in St. Charles County," *Booklist Online* (Dec. 1, 2011).

Chapter Seven

Writer-in-Residence Programs and Awards

Certainly anyone associated with books, be it librarians, writers, bookstore owners (Does anyone know one? Have any been sighted lately?), or avid readers, has heard of writer-in-residence programs. The ones we have knowledge of generally are affiliated with colleges, universities, or even community colleges: in academic settings, in other words. A poet, playwright, or fiction writer temporarily joins the faculty, linking his name to the writing department, and teaches a course and gives a reading. Some of these residences become more or less permanent, as if the writing department is saying, "Here is our featured instructor." The writer-in-residence concept has sprung up in the public library world. What is requested of an author who is appointed to the position varies in degrees and matter, but a prototypical program is offered by the Public Library of Cincinnati and Hamilton County. Application information is easily obtained on the Internet.

I must say that I believe this is a great bang-for-your-buck type of program. A library, especially a relatively small or medium-sized library, can gain great public relations credit in the community by letting everyone possible know that this very admirable program goes on—annually, hopefully—in the local public library. Sponsoring a writer-in-residence program is grown-up stuff; its smacks of sophisticated programming.

The first step in creating your own writer-in-residence program at your library is coming up with financing. I suggest you attempt to get the program endowed by an individual in the community, or the local chamber of commerce, or any local organization that would appreciate seeing its name associated with such an honorable endeavor.

As you will see when you call up the information about the Cincinnati program, one of the requirements to be considered a candidate for an author program is that the author lives in the area. Not only does that requirement provide great support to the local writing community, but it also precludes the library from having to house the author for the event's duration. (A night or two in a hotel may be necessary, depending on the time in the morning or evening that the community events or library promotion events are to take place, as well as how distant from the events the author actually lives.)

Otherwise, it is a superior way to promote local writers as well as your library—the latter in a special, unique, hospitable, community-conscious way.

Look, also, online for guidelines for the Graves Library Writer-in-Residence program in Maine, the Children's Writer-in-Residence fellowship at the Boston Public Library, and Northhampton (MA) Public Library's residency program, and to gather good material for launching your own residency program.

This has the potential for being one of the most exciting author events your library can establish and maintain. Let me reiterate: a writer-in-residence program provides wonderfully effective public relations (showing your community just how proactive and involved your library is in building rapport with the community and supplying highly attractive programs for your book lovers to enjoy); and, of course, supporting the local writer community is "morally" commendable for a public library to engage in.

Author Awards

Let us now turn to an even more "glamorous" connection between a library and a writer; and a step up in terms of the librarian's involvement and participation (meaning, more intense personal and professional effort is needed), but you and your library will be rewarded by basking in the glow of your community's approbation, support, and even surprise.

Follow me as I journey to Tulsa, Oklahoma.

The plane begins its initial descent into Tulsa airport. We are near enough to the city that below us are residential neighborhoods in which houses can be seen as the "individuals" that each house would be seen and recognized at street level.

What struck me from up there, aloft, was the obvious abundance of swimming pools smuggled next to almost every house. I deduced that Tulsa rested comfortably as a community with a significant financial base; and that initial impression would be sustained by what I learned the following day.

I had been invited to Tulsa to present a program—specifically, to lead a workshop—on book reviewing to the public library staff. But only to staff members who were interested and committed enough—brave enough?—to submit to me, in advance of my visit, a mock book review in which each person wrote about a book they had recently read, or even about an old classic that remained a personal favorite. As it turned out, much to my delight, I received a good batch of reviews, ones that I could both compliment and offer constructive criticism of.

I was met at the airport by the adult collection development coordinator at the time at Tulsa City-County Library, Laurie Sundborg. I had met Laurie when she served on the Adult Notable Books Council, a RUSA committee; and at the same time, as adult books editor at *Booklist*, I served as a nonvoting advisor to the committee, basically functioning as the chief justice of procedures. Laurie was accompanied, while waiting for me to arrive and retrieve my bag, by a very pleasant woman, a staff member at the library who had seen my "ad" in *Booklist*, which stated "Would you like the adult books' editor to come to your library to lead a workshop on how to write book reviews for the readers' advisory initiatives at your library?" She suggested to Laurie that I be invited to Tulsa to do just that.

A delightful dinner followed, and then an early turn-in at the hotel where I'd been installed. When Laurie picked me up at the hotel the next morning, and we arrived at the library well in advance of my workshop, she led me on a tour of the building, including both the public and staff-only spaces. She pointed out to me a plaque listing many writers whose names I immediately recognized. "These are the winners of our annual Helmerich Award."

"Explain?"

She did so. It is officially called the Peggy V. Helmerich Distinguished Author Award, a literary prize awarded annually to a highly regarded author who, as the guidelines state, has "written a distinguished body of work and made a major contribution to the field of literature and letters."

Wow. A big deal, obviously. I was further impressed when I asked Laurie if the award involved a monetary component. "Forty thousand dollars," came her response.

I was stunned. This was serious business. I looked again, with more focused eyes, at the list of winners affixed to the wall. The first year of the award was 1985 and the winner was Norman Cousins. The list went on and on with notable writers' names, mostly American but also an Englishman (Ian McEwan), a Canadian (Margaret Atwood), and even an Australian (Thomas Keneally). Giants in U.S.

Q&A

Larry Bartley administers the trust that finances the Peggy V. Helmerich Distinguished Author Award.

From where does the funding for this award come?

An endowment in the Tulsa Library Trust funds the award.

The prize is chosen by whom?

The award is chosen by a committee of community volunteers appointed by the Tulsa Library Trust without any applications from authors, publishers, or outside nominators.

What are the criteria for the award?

The Peggy V. Helmerich Distinguished Author Award was established in 1985 by the Tulsa Library Trust and is given to recognize a distinguished body of work in the field of literature and letters. The Helmerich Award brings outstanding writers to Tulsa to honor their achievements, to benefit the library, and to promote literacy, books, and reading.

For how many years has the award been given?

Thirty-one years.

Tell us about the award reception itself.

The award is given at a black-tie dinner, held at the Central Library, on the first Friday of December. It is followed by a free public presentation and book signing by the author the following morning.

Do you clear the author's ability to attend before actually awarding that particular author the prize?

The authors are invited two years in advance to confirm his/her ability to attend and accept the award.

Who are some of the winners over the years?

The award seeks to recognize the value and importance of outstanding writing of all types and in all fields. In 1985 the first award was given to Norman Cousins followed by writers such as John Updike, Toni Morrison, John le Carré, Norman Mailer, David McCullough, Neil Simon, Joyce Carol Oates, Michael Chabon, Ian McEwan, Ann Patchett, John Grisham, and Rick Atkinson.

letters, such as John Updike, Toni Morrison, Saul Bellow (actually, a Canadian as well) and Eudora Welty occupied places on this amazing list.

For the rest of the tour, and during and immediately after the program I gave, I forgot to pursue with Laurie details of the award; but I had not forgotten it. And when it came time to prepare this book, the Helmerich Award arose in my mind as an interesting—albeit time and energy consuming—author event to bring into my discussion. But, let's face it, as exciting as such a major undertaking—such a major library event within the context of author events—as this kind of award-giving is, it's an event that needs to be annual, needs great financial backing, and requires all kinds of preparation, planning, and execution on the part of the library staff.

In summation, I suggest that if this kind of award/event is of interest to you as a public librarian, you will need to get your administrator fully behind the project, and begin your planning right away; it make a take a year or even a couple years to get all of the organization together to actually launch such an endeavor.

But what a project! For you, for your library, for your community. Good luck.

Chapter Eight

One City One Book Programs

This is the biggie. This is the most involved that a public library and public librarian can get in providing author events and book programs. Google "One City One Book" and you get a workable definition of the concept. "A generic name for a community reading program that attempts to get everyone in a city to read and discuss the same book." In those few words a large cooperative effort is encompassed.

Scroll down the Google search results page and you will see that specific names for the program are often tailored to fit the particular locale: for instance, eastern Connecticut libraries call theirs "One Book One Region," the Winnetka and North-field libraries in suburban Chicago call theirs "One Book, Two Villages," the Iowa Center for the Book, "All Iowa Reads," the counties in western New York, "A Tale of Three Counties," and in Cincinnati, "On the Same Page Cincinnati."

So, what we see are program name variations but also how extensive and nationwide is the concept and practice of one city one book.

Nancy Pearl, at Seattle Public Library at the time, launched the first one-city one-book program from her hometown library in 1998. A bold and amazing concept, to be sure: to get as many citizens of one city to read the same book at the same time and come together to share ideas about it. Might seem impossible; Nancy made it work. And the idea has spread across the country, with one-city, one-book programs now being held annually in many cities. As Nancy has said, "People can go for days at a time not talking to anyone outside their immediate

Q&A

As a way to understand the direct application of the principles of One Book, One City programming, especially for a smaller library, I spoke to **Magan Szwarek,** currently Adult Services Manager, Forest Park Public Library. Previously, at Aurora PL, she was the Popular Materials & Readers' Advisory Specialist.

How many years did you participate in one-book programs at Aurora? Is it an ongoing library project or was it intended to have a limited run?

I participated in four of APL's community read programs, Fox Valley Reads, from 2010–2013. The project began in 2006 and was a partnership among several of the libraries in the area. At the end of the 2013 event the decision was made to put Fox Valley Reads on indefinite hiatus.

Tell me how the program at Aurora got organized. How involved was the city government? Did you follow any specific guidelines found online or suggested by other public librarians?

The program was born out of a desire to launch a One Book, One City reading program, ala Chicago Public Library. The city wasn't involved in the organization at all, to my knowledge, rather it was the heads of adult services at APL, the Messenger Library of North Aurora and Oswego Public Library that collaborated on a NEH Big Read Grant. In subsequent years, themes were chosen and another NEH grant wasn't sought until 2013. The program's organization grew organ-

ically after that first year, loosely based on the grant requirements of the NEH. A typical program would run a little over a month and include between twenty to thirty themed programs, in addition to the discussions of the books.

What problems were encountered in keeping the program going?

The most persistent problem was generating enough community interest to justify the expense, of mounting the program in years that grant funding wasn't sought. The challenge was always to get enough participation to justify the continued effort and budget outlay.

Who selected the "one book" and what were the criteria?

A committee of representatives from each participating library selected the titles. The criteria varied from year to year, based on the program (in some years a theme celebrating a milestone or anniversary was decided and books that related were considered), but availability, the title had to be available in large print, audio and in Spanish translation, readability and mass appeal, and the availability of the author for potential programming were the primary criteria.

What particular audience did APL keep in mind when organizing and presenting a one-city program?

In addition to the traditional book discussion and library program attending audience, we made an effort to keep the Spanish speaking population in mind. During the years I participated children's and teen librarians were added to the committee and related titles and programming were included.

Did the program benefit the library and the community simultaneously and equally? Did the program live up to expectations?

I'd like to think the benefits were equally distributed between the community and the library. Certainly, the experience of planning and executing the ambitious slate of programs was beneficial to the library staff involved and the programs themselves were enriching, entertaining and aligned with the missions of the libraries involved. The challenge of advertising the program, making people aware that it was happening at all, and generating community participation kept Fox Valley Reads from making as large an impact as it could have, which was disappointing and, ultimately, led to its demise.

◇◇◇◇◇◇◇◇◇◇◇◇◇◇◇◇◇◇◇◇◇◇◇◇◇◇◇◇◇◇◇◇◇◇

family. There are precious few opportunities for people of different ethnic backgrounds, economic levels, or ages to sit down together and discuss ideas that are important to them; this project provides that opportunity."

To get a more personal idea of how the plan works, let's follow a recent announcement in Chicago of an installment of the concept. As Arts and Entertainment reporter from *Show Me Chicago* blog Carole Kuhrt Brewer so aptly stated it, "One Book, One Chicago, launched in 2001, has become a popular program that focuses on a single book through a series of events and activities offered in every neighborhood across the city, creating a citywide book club."[1] And that is the guiding philosophy behind all such programs.

The season in Chicago runs from October through the following spring. The 2014–2015 selection was *The Amazing Adventures of Kavalier & Clay* by the highly regarded contemporary American fiction writer Michael Chabon. It was, in my estimation, an inspired choice. Chabon is highly literary—appealing to the more snobbish readers who don't want to involve themselves in a watered-down read for the masses. But by revealing an immaculate and humorous and delightfully offbeat understanding of human nature, at the same time that he's proving his literary bona fides, he's telling highly creative and greatly spirited—and thus compelling—tales with characters who are eccentric but not beyond the reach of the appreciation by every reader. In other words, he's a writer for everyone, which is certainly necessary for a one-book one-city choice. Not high-falutin' literary but not bottom-line pedestrian, either; somewhere in the middle, with leanings toward the literary side. (After all, the point of the program is not only to draw a community together but also to raise appreciation of books and what they can teach people about life.)

What is readily apparent when reading the promotional materials for Chicago Public Library concerning the 2014–15 One Book, One Chicago season is that it is the theme of *Kavalier & Clay*, rather than the actual plot, that has been identified and used to promote the book and attract participants. This is entirely supportable; the theme, more so than the plot, will draw in the widest range of readers. The theme of *Kavalier & Clay* is presented, succinctly, in the Chicago Public Library press release as "Heroes: Real and Imagined." Basic statement, right? But helpful broadening of this trenchant theme identification is provided further along in the press release with this line: "Joe Kavalier and Sam Clay reimagine and redefine the comic book hero and in the process force us to grapple with questions about heroism: what does a hero look like, why do we need heroes. what makes one a hero—these are only some of the questions with which we struggle alongside Joe and Sammy as they create The Escapist, their greatest comic book hero."

Ah, okay. They've now made the novel sound pretty irresistible, I'd say, and have spread the irresistibility across adult and juvenile readerships.

The season began in October 9 with an in-person interview at the Harold Washington Library Center. The Chicago Public Library press release lists the other events tied to the program, which included exhibits, book discussions, panel discussions, musical performances, and storytelling.

The "mother" of all documents to consult for guidance in this area is a 44-page presentation called "Planning Your Community-Wide Read," compiled by the Public Programs Office of the American Library Association (visit www.ala.org/publicprograms, then, in the search box, type in One Book One Community, and then click on "Planning Your Community-Wide Read"). This is a vastly comprehensive guide, which addresses all kinds of issues and angles and solutions for a community-wide reading program. many of which you undoubtedly had not ever thought of. And this is, of course, the very reason for this document to exist!

The range of ideas and suggestions gathered into this document is startlingly comprehensive. *How to formulate the primary goals of your reading program,* which includes program goals (how will the library benefit?). *Audience goals* (who your program will serve in terms of age levels and demographics). *Thematic goals,* which prods you into thinking about if there are themes that relate to your library or community issues. Community goals—meaning, what issues and agendas are relevant to your community. Entering financial partnerships. Offering a budget worksheet template. Criteria for selecting a book to read (including the helpful thought that a visit by the author is an important part of your program and will greatly impact your book choice). Marketing and promotion, compiling an event checklist, and preparing participant evaluation forms. Not a stone is left unturned. You are ready to embark on the book program of your life!

NOTE

1. Carole Kuhrt Brewer, "One Book, Once Chicago: Book Selection for 2015 Announced." Chicagonow.com/show-me-chicago/2014.

INDEX